ADVANCE PRAISE

"What I find most compelling about this book is the compassion and warmth that accompany the reader's journey from hiding and isolation, hallmarks of trauma and addiction, to openness and self-acceptance. It's a journey that passes through many landscapes, including the scientific foundation of bodily health, cultural distinctions in our understanding of risk, and modes of thought and action that cultivate trust, both of ourselves and of others.

This book takes focusing on the road, from a conceptual understanding—of, indeed, a bodily exploration—to a fluid (meta-focusing), intuition-guided methodology that links urgent needs to real solutions, concretely defined, and available either in therapy or outside of therapy. Grounded in the body's urge for self-care, Winhall's exercises offer a remarkable pathway through emotional healing."

—**Marc Lewis, PhD, C. Psych,** professor emeritus of developmental psychology and neuroscience, University of Toronto, and clinical psychologist

"Jan Winhall highlights the vital importance of drawing on one's inner wisdom when healing from trauma and addiction. This work empowers both trauma clinicians and survivors and instills hope in those who are healing from trauma."

—**Ruth A. Lanius, MD, PhD,** professor of psychiatry, director of the Posttraumatic Stress Disorder (PTSD) Research Unit, and Harris-Woodman Chair, University of Western Ontario

"Jan Winhall has a remarkable way of taking complex subjects and grounding them in practical, healing strategies that work. She invites you to relate to addictions as learned habits that can be unlearned. Rooted in trauma-informed care and Polyvagal Theory, Winhall provides a compassionate understanding of how addictive behaviors were developed as the best-known attempts to manage adverse life events and the resulting dysregulated nervous system. Here, you are skillfully guided through the felt sense approach to reduce the harm of addictions while enhancing your capacity for joy!"

—**Dr. Arielle Schwartz**, clinical psychologist and author of *The Complex PTSD Workbook*

"Jan Winhall's new guidebook is brimming with enlightened, effective strategies for addressing the deeply interwoven challenges of treating trauma and addiction. Centered by the Four Circles Harm Reduction Practice, her body-centered model of 20 practices is bolstered by an insightful theoretical foundation combined with deep respect for the wisdom of the body to release self-acceptance and healing. Organized with a gentle, grounded, step-by-step approach, this book will become an inspirational companion for therapists and their clients searching for an innovative, nonjudgmental paradigm for addressing addictive processes and underlying trauma."

—**Cece Sykes, LCSW,** consultant, senior international trainer, Internal Family Systems Institute, and coauthor of *Internal Family Systems for Addiction: Trauma-Informed, Compassion-Based Interventions for Substance Use, Eating, Gambling and More*

20 Embodied Practices for Healing Trauma and Addiction

THE NORTON SERIES ON INTERPERSONAL NEUROBIOLOGY

Louis Cozolino, PhD, Series Editor
Allan N. Schore, PhD, Series Editor (2007–2014)
Daniel J. Siegel, MD, Founding Editor

The field of mental health is in a tremendously exciting period of growth and conceptual reorganization. Independent findings from a variety of scientific endeavors are converging in an interdisciplinary view of the mind and mental well-being. An interpersonal neurobiology of human development enables us to understand that the structure and function of the mind and brain are shaped by experiences, especially those involving emotional relationships.

The Norton Series on Interpersonal Neurobiology provides cutting-edge, multidisciplinary views that further our understanding of the complex neurobiology of the human mind. By drawing on a wide range of traditionally independent fields of research—such as neurobiology, genetics, memory, attachment, complex systems, anthropology, and evolutionary psychology—these texts offer mental health professionals a review and synthesis of scientific findings often inaccessible to clinicians. The books advance our understanding of human experience by finding the unity of knowledge, or consilience, that emerges with the translation of findings from numerous domains of study into a common language and conceptual framework. The series integrates the best of modern science with the healing art of psychotherapy.

20 EMBODIED PRACTICES FOR HEALING TRAUMA AND ADDICTION

USING THE FELT SENSE POLYVAGAL MODEL

JAN WINHALL

Norton Professional Books

An Imprint of W. W. Norton & Company
Independent Publishers Since 1923

Note to Readers: This book is intended as a general information resource for professionals practicing in the field of psychotherapy and mental health. It is not a substitute for appropriate training or clinical supervision. Standards of clinical practice and protocol vary in different practice settings and change over time. No technique or recommendation is guaranteed to be safe or effective in all circumstances, and neither the publisher nor the author(s) can guarantee the complete accuracy, efficacy, or appropriateness of any particular recommendation in every respect or in all settings or circumstances.

Any URLs displayed in this book link or refer to websites that existed as of press time. The publisher is not responsible for, and should not be deemed to endorse or recommend, any website other than its own or any content that it did not create. The author, also, is not responsible for any third-party material.

For my mother, whose feminist
spirit lives on in this liberatory work.

CONTENTS

Acknowledgments   11
Foreword by Stephen W. Porges   15
Introduction   19

CHAPTER 1: Creating a Safe Nest (Practices 1–3)   33

CHAPTER 2: Finding Safety in the Body: The Felt
      Sense Polyvagal Model (Practices 4–5)   47

CHAPTER 3: Polyvagal Informed Focusing and
      the Felt Sense (Practices 6–9)   65

CHAPTER 4: The Very Bad Habit of Addiction
      (Practices 10–12)   85

CHAPTER 5: The Underbelly of Addiction:
      Trauma and Attachment (Practices 13–14)   111

CHAPTER 6: Deepening Your Trauma Story:
      Meeting Isabella (Practices 15–17)   131

CHAPTER 7: Empowerment: Connection and
      Community (Practices 18–20)   151

Conclusion   167
Appendix   169
References   171
Index   177

ACKNOWLEDGMENTS

First and foremost, I want to acknowledge Steve Porges. Steve, you have given us a profound gift in your new, trauma-informed understanding of the autonomic nervous system. It enables us as trauma and addiction therapists to reframe the manifestations of trauma as adaptive features of a dysregulated nervous system. This paradigm shift elevates somatic therapies by bringing body wisdom to the forefront of healing modalities. While other cultures and therapies have recognized the wisdom of the body, your contribution continues to have a profound impact on the current cognitive-oriented therapies that have dominated the Western world.

Your mentorship and continuous accessibility have enabled me to flourish. Connecting me with the right people has brought this book to life. Thanks to you I met your editor at Norton, Deborah Malmud.

Deborah, your belief in this project made all the difference! You supported the unique approach that this book takes in asking readers to find a partner and/or therapist to engage in the 20 embodied practices together. Thank you for supporting my deeply held belief that people struggling with trauma and addiction need to connect and heal together. I couldn't have written this book any other way.

A profound thank you to Eugene Gendlin, my somatic teacher for over 30 years. You mastered the art of "being with" another person in a way that I have not seen in others. As a philosopher and psychologist, your contribution is unsurpassed. I carry the felt sense of your teachings in my body, and I am eternally grateful to you.

To Mary Armstrong, gifted trauma therapist and student of Gendlin's: I learned how to hone the skills of focusing from you, dear Mary.

To my beautiful polyvagal community: I feel so lucky to be a part of this rich and warm circle. Each one of you helped me to bring this work to life. Special thanks to:

Randall, you are my shore. As I go out to explore, I return to connect with you. Thank you for being there in such a deep and nurturing way.

Michael, polyvagal pal, we are navigating the terrain, and keeping each other company on this amazing adventure. Love you.

Blake, thank you for all your guidance in shaping the remarkable training program that we have developed over several years of working together. And thank you for a wonderful friendship!

Suzie, thank you for your warmth, support, and guidance in shaping this work. I am looking forward to getting to know you better as time goes on.

Stephanie, it is always fun to work together in shaping our polyvagal community. You understand the profound importance of coregulation. Your energy and commitment is wonderful.

Caroline, I so appreciate your knowledge in marketing new ideas. You are always so helpful and encouraging.

Jen, your gentle guidance in all things related to customer care is so important. You know how to create a safely held container for our students. I value this so much!

Jerry, you gave me my start in the media world. You were the one who helped me to feel comfortable in the recording studio. Your gentle presence is a gift. It warms my heart. Thank you so much for believing in me!

Arielle, you are such a delight, such a truly gifted and generous person. I look forward to making more things happen together!

Serge, your abiding friendship and introduction to Steve is a blessing.

Mel, thank you for being open to diverse ways of thinking, and for your warm and playful presence. More collaboration to come.

Thank you to all our international partners, Florence and Marc, and others that I am just beginning to know. It is thrilling to be part of forming a worldwide movement. I love connecting and teaching in your communities.

To my students, you know who you are! You are my cocreators. The work deepens with you and me in dialogue with each other. Without coregulation, it would not be the same. This book will allow us to grow and create more community across the world. Deep gratitude for you, always!

To my Focusing community, thank you for continuing to spread the word about Focusing. A special thank you to Nancy Falls who joins me in her expert teaching of Polyvagal Informed Focusing, and to Leslie Ellis whose guest teaching in my FSPM course carries Gendlin's work forward in a profound way.

For my web designer and assistant, Rachan Chindarsi, a big, wide thank you for helping me in our day-to-day and ever-expanding work. Your gentle, compassionate way with students is much appreciated. Your guidance in marketing and all related things is invaluable.

For my family, who has supported this work through reading, talking, hugging, and eating many delicious meals together, I love you. I watch with pride as my children, Marika, whose work is in these pages, and my son, Peter, continue their own contributions to our field. I confess I am reliant on my husband, Tony Cohn, for his intelligent first reading of the manuscript and his enduring and essential technical help.

For the women in my first trauma group, this work had its beginning with you. I will always be grateful for your trust in me.

The wider feminist community knew the wisdom of seeking safety in the body. Thank you for steering me in the right direction, teaching me the gift of embodied presence.

For all of you who have shared your journeys with me, know that you have helped make this book what it is.

And finally, for you, dear reader, as you engage and unfold, I want to acknowledge your journey and thank you for bringing me into your world. This book is for you!

FOREWORD

By Stephen W. Porges

Trauma and addiction are persistent challenges in both clinical and personal spheres, deeply intertwined with our nervous system, emotions, and bodily experiences. Their complexity often makes them resistant to purely cognitive or behavioral interventions. In *20 Embodied Practices for Healing Trauma and Addiction*, Jan Winhall offers a fresh perspective on healing through her innovative Felt Sense Polyvagal Model (FSPM). This model integrates the body's wisdom, using embodied practices to foster recovery and resilience.

As the creator of Polyvagal Theory, I am grateful to see how Winhall seamlessly integrates my work with Eugene Gendlin's concept of the "felt sense." Her approach expands upon the importance of the autonomic nervous system (ANS) in our sense of safety and well-being. Through decades of therapeutic practice, Winhall has developed a model that rethinks conventional treatments for trauma and addiction, guiding individuals toward restoration by utilizing the body's inherent capacity for healing.

In her previous book, *Treating Trauma and Addiction with the Felt Sense Polyvagal Model*, Winhall introduced the theoretical foundation of this framework. Now, in this book, she takes the next step by offering clinicians and clients a set of practical, accessible tools for healing. These embodied practices are designed to help individuals reconnect with their bodies, regulate their nervous systems, and, crucially, rediscover a sense of safety essential for the healing process.

At the heart of the Felt Sense Polyvagal Model (FSPM) is a transformative shift in how we understand trauma and addiction. Rather than seeing trauma as pathology or disorder, the FSPM reframes it as an adaptive response—an attempt by the ANS to protect us when safety is compromised. Addiction, too, is reframed not as a moral failing but as a state regulation strategy—a survival tool in the absence of safety. This compassionate reframe liberates us from the stigma associated with trauma and addiction, allowing us to recognize that our body's responses are efforts to cope with unsafe environments. With this understanding, Winhall invites readers to embark on a journey of healing, guided by 20 embodied practices that offer pathways to self-regulation and well-being.

Central to the Felt Sense Polyvagal Model is the role of neuroception—the unconscious detection of safety or threat by the autonomic nervous system. This concept, drawn from Polyvagal Theory, explains how our body constantly scans the environment for cues, determining whether we are safe or in danger. When our nervous system detects safety, we enter a ventral vagal state characterized by calmness, connection, and growth. However, when threats are perceived, survival states such as fight, flight, or freeze take over. Chronic exposure to these survival states, as seen in trauma and addiction, creates dysregulation that keeps us trapped. Winhall's model helps break this cycle by teaching embodied practices that bring the nervous system back into regulation.

Winhall incorporates Gendlin's concept of the felt sense, a bodily awareness that provides deeper insight into our internal experiences. Gendlin emphasized that real change occurs when we connect with this felt sense, allowing for a shift in how we experience ourselves and the world. The FSPM uniquely merges this idea with Polyvagal Theory, showing how the felt sense can guide us into a more regulated, ventral vagal state where healing becomes possible.

The practices in this book are built upon four key concepts. First, the autonomic nervous system is the primary source of healing, as trauma and addiction stem from shifts in ANS states. Second, trauma and addiction are adaptive responses, representing the body's best attempt to protect itself when safety is lacking. Third, addiction functions as a state regulation strategy, an effort to manage overwhelming emotions and sensations. Finally, Gendlin's felt sense is central to healing, signaling a shift from defensive states to grounded, connected ones.

Winhall's integration of various frameworks—Polyvagal Theory, Focusing, trauma-informed and feminist perspectives, interpersonal neurobiology, and the learning model of addiction—provides a comprehensive foundation for understanding trauma and addiction. She moves beyond the pathology-based models and instead presents addiction as a response to unsafe environments. By viewing addiction through this compassionate lens, she removes the stigma and empowers individuals to reclaim their bodies and lives.

The 20 embodied practices shared in this book are accessible, concrete tools designed for both personal use and therapeutic settings. Each practice invites individuals to tune into their body's felt sense, recognize the state of their nervous system, and gently shift toward a more regulated state. These practices include breathwork, mindfulness, movement, and other somatic exercises that reestablish a sense of safety in the body. Through regular use, individuals can create lasting shifts in their autonomic patterns, moving away from survival states and toward healing and connection.

A core theme of the book is that true healing does not come from symptom management or behavior control, but from reconnecting with the body's wisdom. Trauma often disconnects us from our bodies, making it difficult to feel or trust our internal signals. Winhall's practices help restore this connection, empowering individuals to feel safe enough to explore their inner world and begin healing.

A major strength of Winhall's model is its emphasis on coregulation—healing through safe, supportive relationships. Trauma often damages our ability to trust others, leaving us isolated. The practices in this book help individuals not only self-regulate but also build healthy, safe connections with others. Coregulation plays a critical role in recovery, as healing cannot happen in isolation; it occurs within the context of supportive relationships.

Ultimately, *20 Embodied Practices for Healing Trauma and Addiction* is a profound guide to reclaiming one's body, life, and sense of self. By listening to the wisdom of our bodies and cultivating a sense of safety, we can break free from the cycles of trauma and addiction that have held us back. Winhall's book offers both hope and practical tools for those on this healing journey, transforming how we view and address trauma and addiction.

I invite readers to approach this book with curiosity, openness, and self-compassion. The embodied practices that Winhall offers provide valuable steps toward self-regulation, safety, and connection, not only in recovery but in living a more integrated and connected life.

As you engage with this work, remember that healing is not about fixing what is broken—it's about reconnecting with the parts of yourself that have been disconnected by trauma. By honoring the wisdom of your body, you can begin to move toward a life of greater freedom, health, and well-being.

Introduction

Chances are if you are with me now, holding my book in your hands, you are curious about a new way of understanding and healing from trauma and addiction. You could have chosen lots of other books that talk about learning new skills and changing thought patterns. While we will be doing that, the primary source of healing in the Felt Sense Polyvagal Model (FSPM) comes from the body and its innate way of finding new grounded neuropathways for healing.

Increasing numbers of people are experiencing significant trauma responses and turning to addictive behaviors to manage anxiety and depression. We are living in very unsettling times. In addition to day-to-day problems, lingering trauma caused by the COVID-19 pandemic, escalating wars, and climate change are challenging us beyond our capacity to cope. Many of you are spinning around in treatment programs that are not effective. Our disease model is failing us.

While this top-down cognitive behavioral approach has contributed to a wide range of discoveries, we miss the mark when we apply these methods without integrating a bottom-up approach that incorporates our bodies' innate capacity to heal. When we treat the body as one whole living organism, we see how mind and body are designed to complement each other. Ironically, new developments in neuroscience achieved through a top-down methodology are aiding in the understanding and appreciation of how trauma and addiction impact the body. The Felt Sense Polyvagal Model (FSPM) offers a new way of understanding traumatic responses as *our body's attempt to protect us* when we don't feel safe. It's quite a shift in thinking, and it offers much hope in healing. It is this hope that we will take with us as we begin our journey together.

This book is based on my book for clinicians and other mental health professionals, *Treating Trauma and Addiction with the Felt Sense Polyvagal Model* (2021). It's designed to be read by professionals and their clients. While this book can be read on its own, a more detailed description of the model in the clinician book can be helpful for therapists and clients alike.

We start with a brief description of the five theories that form the foundation of the model. Subsequent chapters describe aspects of the theories and offer *20 embodied practices* that create a step-by-step path that can be used either individually or in group settings. Together therapist and client can formulate and implement a unique and embodied harm reduction plan that is grounded in research and at the cutting edge of trauma and addiction recovery.

This book will help you:

1. Manage distressful emotions and physical sensations to preempt trauma/addictive behaviors.
2. Create a well-paced and structured lifestyle.
3. Engage in healthy, meaningful relationships.
4. Live a life of integrity, where your values align with your behaviors.

FIVE THEORIES

The Felt Sense Polyvagal Model was developed over 40 years of practicing as a trauma therapist. It began with my experience in leading a women's group for sexual abuse survivors in the early 1980s. The foundation of the model is based on five theories that build on each other. Each theory can be thought of as a different "story" that helps you understand more about yourself and your troubling behavior. As you read about each "story" you may find that a light bulb moment occurs as you see yourself in the description. Suddenly your "crazy" behavior starts to make sense! The five theories that we will explore include feminist and trauma-informed theory, felt sense/Focusing, interpersonal neurobiology, a learning model of addiction, and Polyvagal Theory.

FEMINIST AND TRAUMA-INFORMED THEORY: WHAT HELPED YOU NOW HARMS YOU

The problem survivors experience with their bodies . . . splitting,
numbing, addictions, began as attempts to survive. You cut off
from your body for good reasons, but now you need to heal . . . to
move from estrangement from the body to integration.
—BASS & DAVIS, *THE COURAGE TO HEAL*, 1988, P. 208

Traditional therapy focuses on talking, sharing, and understanding events. This is an important part of the process, but there is another more powerful language that is being overlooked, the language of the body. While you are struggling to change the way you think and feel, your body keeps engaging in repetitive trauma responses that become more and more habitual. No matter how hard you try to think or will your way out of it, your body leads you back to behaviors that help you in the short term but harm you in the long term. It then becomes easy to blame these bodily responses—to see them as a sickness, or weakness. Often a power struggle ensues, with you pitted against your body's response of craving, or numbing out.

What is less understood, but vitally important to appreciate, is that the body responds with dissociation and addictive behaviors for a very good reason. Early feminist healers like Bass and Davis, quoted above, understood this. In their book *The Courage to Heal*, they suggest that survivors "cut off from their bodies" as an adaptive attempt to cope when there is no escape from unbearable pain (1988).

It's very powerful to realize that **these behaviors are adaptive in mal-adaptive environments**. Let's pause here and really take this in. It means that your trauma/addiction behaviors once saved you. And you are not crazy because you engage in them. In fact, they are instinctual ways for your body to protect you when there is no perceived escape. Unfortunately, even when our environment becomes safe, we can get locked in old dissociative and addictive patterns. That's where body-based practices like the ones you will learn in this book, can help you heal by regulating your physiology, your body's response to threat.

When we listen freshly, without preconceived interpretations and diagnostic categories, we appreciate how we are designed to survive. We shift the paradigm so that instead of viewing addiction and other trauma responses as diseases, we understand them as heroic attempts to bear the unbearable. Instead of being locked in a power struggle, you appreciate your body's wisdom. This under-standing creates a "light bulb moment." It liberates you from shame and blame as you begin to truly believe that your body is simply doing what it is designed to do. This belief forms the foundation of the FSPM. As you take it in you can begin to rest in the knowledge that connecting with your body is the doorway to liberation.

Judith Herman (*Trauma and Recovery*, 1992) a feminist psychiatrist from Bos-ton, helps us to understand the paradoxical behavior of survivors when engaging in self-harming/self-soothing behaviors.

> Abused children generally discover at some point in their development that they can produce major, though temporary, alterations in their affective state by vol-untarily inducing autonomic crisis or extreme autonomic arousal. Purging and vomiting, compulsive sexual behavior, compulsive risk taking, or exposure to danger, and the use of psychoactive drugs become the vehicles by which abused children attempt to regulate their internal emotional states. Through these devices, abused children attempt to obliterate their chronic dysphoria and to simulate, however briefly, an internal state of well-being and comfort that cannot otherwise be achieved. (Herman, 1992, p. 109)

Herman makes a very important point in her reference to the autonomic ner-vous system (ANS). This is the part of the body that monitors how safe we feel. You will be familiar with it as a flight/fight/freeze and shutdown state in your body. She suggests that these compulsive devices act as an attempt to shift inter-nal autonomic states to seek comfort. As we shall see, Herman's insight into the function of self-harming behaviors through the ANS foreshadows the work of Porges's Polyvagal Theory of addiction.

Within the feminist community, prioritizing safety is a first step in the heal-ing journey. Herman stressed the importance of titrating the therapy process. She suggested a three-stage model: (1) establishing safety; (2) remembering and mourning; (3) reconnection. This book will follow her process, starting with Chapter 1, "Creating a Safe Nest."

FOCUSING/FELT SENSING: AN INTEROCEPTIVE PROCESS

The Felt Sense Polyvagal Model uses *Focusing*, or *felt sensing* as it is sometimes called, as the doorway into embodied knowing. This is an interoceptive process, meaning it connects us with awareness of bodily sensation and emotions. Focusing helps us connect with a deep, quiet place inside. When we pause and bring attention down into the center of the body, we begin to access a deeper knowing about how we are living our lives. It is the *still, quiet voice inside* that knows something more about the situation that we are in. Sometimes this knowing comes in a physical sensation. A tight sensation in the chest may soften as you learn to welcome your fear or sadness. Honoring your uncomfortable feelings is the pathway to healing. Because addiction and trauma may have made it unsafe to connect with the body, we take our time, slowly dipping in and out of deeper awareness.

Focusing began at the University of Chicago in the 1950s. Gene Gendlin, father of the Felt Sense, was studying with Carl Rogers, a famous American psychologist. They were fascinated with understanding how people change in psychotherapy, so they conducted research studies asking clients and therapists who reported positive outcomes to share their process. Thousands of hours of recordings revealed that people paused during the sessions. When Gendlin asked what they were doing as they paused, they shared that they were quietly connecting down into their bodies, listening to how it felt inside (1978/1981). He named this process of connecting inside "Focusing." As they paid attention to their bodies, clients became aware of their thoughts, feelings, physical sensations, and memories. In this integrated state a whole sense of the situation would form. He called this the "felt sense."

Felt Shift

As the session progressed and clients felt connected with a compassionate therapist as their guide, something new would often come, something that they didn't already know about their issue. It was as if the body was waiting for a quiet, safe space in which to reveal a deeper knowing of the issue. This "aha" moment was accompanied by a release of physical tension, often coming with tears, or sometimes laughter. Gendlin called this the "felt shift," the body's "motor of change" (1978/1981). This shift points us toward safety and growth.

Gendlin noted that although nothing had changed with the problem, it felt much clearer and more manageable. This felt shift is the most important aspect of Focusing.

When we get stuck in trauma and addiction states, we deaden the felt sense and the felt shift. In the service of survival, we wither, losing the very best of life's experiences. Our Focusing practice invites the body to reawaken, connecting us with body wisdom, our guide in the healing journey.

Six Steps

Gendlin wanted everyone to be able to access the felt sense, so he created a six-step process that he called Foc ·sing (1978/1981). The 20 embodied practices in this book use the six steps to help you learn how to access a greater connection with yourself and those around you.

INTERPERSONAL NEUROBIOLOGY

Exciting developments arose in the field of trauma in the 1990s. It became known as the "decade of the brain." New technology like pet scans and fMRIs allowed researchers to see into the brain. This has had a big impact on how we understand the biology of trauma. During this time, Dan Siegel developed a model for working with trauma that integrated the latest findings in neurobiology with the process of interpersonal relationships, which he called Interpersonal Neurobiology (IPNB) (1999).

This integration contributed to our field by offering a new strength-based paradigm. Rather than viewing behavior through a pathological lens, Siegel suggests that all diagnoses can be viewed through the lens of emotional regulation. The more traumatized we are the more we shift into dysregulated states that interrupt our capacity to be integrated, to feel whole and present. Siegel contributed to our understanding of how early attachment with caregivers impacts these states of dysregulation. We will explore how childhood experiences have shaped you and your capacity to calm yourself.

Siegel's theory is complex but can be broken down into bite size pieces that form the basis of understanding how mind and body relate to each other. He created a practice called Mindsight as part of developing new neuropathways to tap into the felt sense (Siegel, 2010).

LEARNING MODEL OF ADDICTION

There are many ways that cultures have understood addiction: It's a moral failing, it's a brain disease, it's a quest for self-medicating, it's a result of childhood attachment trauma. The FSPM is based on Marc Lewis's learning model of addiction (2015). Lewis describes addictions as bad habits that follow the same neuropathways as any other kind of learning. He gave the example of falling in love. In this euphoric state our brain is consumed by thinking about the person, planning the next visit, waiting for the phone to ring, much like the state of addiction. The neuropathways in the brain look the same, yet we don't think of being in love as a disease.

We will examine how addiction works in the brain and how we can heal by rewiring our trauma/addictive neuropathways. The learning model is based on the concept of neuroplasticity—the brain's capacity to change and grow. This knowledge helps us to realize how the 20 practices in this book are literally building new neuropathways of health and safety in your brain. The more you engage in the practices, the more you can sustain a healing lifestyle. This is empowering! So how to define addiction in this new light?

> Addiction: It helps you in the short term, hurts you in the long term, and you can't stop doing it.
>
> —JAN WINHALL, M.S.W.

This simple definition is without judgement about the origins of addiction and is inclusive of all behaviors or substances that constitute an addiction. If you are unsure about whether your behavior is addictive you can ask yourself if it is helping you in the short term, hurting you in the long term, and are you able to stop doing it? And if you can stop, do you inevitably start again?

POLYVAGAL THEORY: SAFETY IS OUR NORTH STAR

The Vagus Nerve as the Brain/Body Connector

Polyvagal Theory, created by Stephen Porges (2011), is the study of the ANS, the linked massive network of nerve fibers that make up the vagus nerve. The vagus is a long cranial nerve that runs through the center of your body, up to your ears and into your facial muscles. It acts as a bidirectional pathway carrying information from areas such as your gut, stomach, lungs, heart, facial muscles, and ears to your brainstem.

When we feel safe enough, the ventral branch of the vagus nerve is activated. This is the part of the vagus that is located above the diaphragm. In this grounded state we experience health, growth, and restoration, the full felt sense of lived experience.

The Power of Neuroception

Through a process Porges calls *neuroception*, our autonomic nervous system monitors our sense of safety and unconsciously shifts us from a ventral state into flight/fight, freeze, and shutdown states to protect us. Perhaps because we are not consciously aware of this process, and because Western culture emphasizes thinking over feeling, we tend to minimize the importance of the ANS. But we make a big mistake when we do this because our ANS state defines how we are experiencing our life.

Let's pause and think about this. Life is completely different depending on whether we are feeling safe, enraged, happy, terrified, lonely, or depressed. Our state colors our thoughts, feelings, physical sensations, and our behaviors. Developing the capacity to pause enables us to become aware of what state we are in. This is turn helps us to make better choices in how we respond. This is key in liberating us from unconsciously falling into old trauma and addictive behaviors.

The Dorsal Vagus

Another important part of Polyvagal Theory comes from Porges's discovery of another pathway of the vagus nerve that hadn't been included in our traditional model of the ANS. He calls this the *dorsal vagus* (2019). It is responsible for the state that comes *after* freeze. It is a shutdown, dissociative, numb state. No wonder trauma therapists were amazed at this discovery. We see this state in our clients all the time. I bet this describes how you've felt before too. When life becomes overwhelming and it feels like there is no escape, our neuroceptive process unconsciously shifts the body into dissociative and addictive states to bring relief in the numbing oblivion of the dorsal vagus.

Self-Harm and Addictions From a Polyvagal Lens

Herman's insight into the role of self-harming and addictive behaviors as ways of shifting states in the ANS was an important starting point. Porges's addition of the dorsal vagus as a pathway in our ANS adds an essential piece of the puzzle. Now we have a name for the state that brings dissociated relief.

Self-harming and addictive behaviors can now be understood as state regulation strategies that shift the body from a flight/fight state to a shutting down dorsal state and back again. The need to shift states is not conscious but driven by a foundational need for survival. When the body becomes stuck in a dorsal numb state it looks for ways to move away from these negative feelings. Addictions are very effective ways to shift back into a flight/fight state.

Trauma Feedback Loop (TFL)

This path of flight/fight, freeze, and shutdown forms a feedback loop. The more the body repeats these behaviors, the more the brain develops a trauma feedback loop neuropathway. What becomes very clear is that the grounded branch of the vagus nerve, the ventral branch, is not available in the trauma loop. We've lost our felt sense of life.

When we are stuck in the TFL we can develop faulty neuroception, meaning that we misread safe enough experiences as triggers of old trauma. This can lead to more need for self-harm and addictive behaviors in an unsuccessful attempt to bring emotional and physical regulation into the body. This is a vicious circle indeed.

It is important to note that trauma and addictive behaviors do not occur when we are in a safe, regulated state in our nervous system. Therefore, the path to healing starts with establishing enough safety. Twenty embodied practices are involved in the activation of the ventral branch of the vagus nerve, engaging your body's natural desire to heal. One of these practices, the Four Circle Harm Reduction Practice, is presented as the framework for healing from addictive behaviors.

Interoception/Neuroception: The Felt Sense Polyvagal Model

Understanding how neuroception guides our body into shifting states helps to understand how *interoception*, a felt sense process, is involved in state regulation. The Felt Sense Polyvagal model posits that the felt shift described in the Focusing steps is accompanied by a shift in the ANS toward a more ventral, grounded state. These two embodied processes work in collaboration, carrying the body forward into the fullness of life.

FOUR CORE CONCEPTS EMERGE

1. **The ANS is our main source of healing.** The autonomic nervous system is responsible for monitoring our sense of safety. When the body is in a ventral state of safety, trauma and addiction responses don't occur. Therefore, a main focus in therapy is to practice neural exercises that promote ventral pathways.
2. **Trauma/addiction responses are adaptive in maladaptive contexts.** These behaviors are the body's way of protecting us. Rather than "disorders" they are in fact a very ordered way of adapting when there is not enough perceived safety. When we get stuck in trauma feedback loops, we need to use our embodied practices.
3. **Addictions serve as propellers in the ANS because they shift the body back and forth from flight/fight, to freeze, to shutting down.** Porges calls addictions "state regulation strategies" since they function as strategies for coping with dysregulated states. A common example of this is using alcohol to shift from flight/fight to a numbing shutdown response (Winhall & Porges, 2022).
4. **The felt shift is a shift in the ANS.** Physical changes are also linked to the felt sense. Sometimes when Focusing, people will experience a felt shift, a physical release/relief in the body. This felt shift is accompanied by ANS shift into a more ventral state.

TWENTY EMBODIED PRACTICES

These four core concepts of the Felt Sense Polyvagal Model form the basis of the 20 embodied practices that are integrated throughout the book. They are based on research and practice across cultures. Using these concepts and practices as our guide, you will learn to honor your body's capacity to monitor safety and find a grounded felt sense. Most of all, you will learn to appreciate your trauma and addiction responses as your body's way to help you be as safe as possible when there is nowhere to hide.

SUMMARY

This introductory chapter presents an overview of the Felt Sense Polyvagal Model (FSPM) as it was developed over 40 years of clinical practice with trauma/ addiction clients. The FSPM challenges the current disease model of addiction. Instead, it offers a new embodied paradigm that views addictions as adaptive state regulation strategies in the autonomic nervous system.

Five theoretical frameworks are briefly introduced including feminist and trauma-informed theory, Focusing/felt sense, interpersonal neurobiology, learning model of addiction, and Polyvagal Theory. The two embodied processes of neuroception and interoception form the basis of the FSPM. A description of the trauma feedback loop is included.

Four core concepts that uphold the model are presented:

1. The ANS is our main source of healing.
2. Trauma/addiction responses are adaptive in maladaptive environments.
3. Addictions serve as propellers in the ANS because they shift the body back and forth from flight/fight, to freeze, to shutting down.
4. The felt shift is a shift in the ANS.

This book takes you through 20 embodied practices of the FSPM that provide a healing path toward health, growth, and restoration.

20 Embodied Practices for Healing Trauma and Addiction

CHAPTER 1

Creating a Safe Nest (Practices 1–3)

We are at the beginning of our journey together. Beginnings can be complex, particularly when we are dealing with trauma and addiction. Maybe you've walked down this path many times in attempting to understand and change your behaviors. Or it may be very new and tender. Notice how it feels to be at the start. Are you anxious, excited, hopeless, or numb? Maybe all the above.

If you are a clinician, body worker, or a coach accompanying your clients with this book, your personal history will be part of your journey too. We bring our heart and soul into the relationships we make. We hear unspeakable things. As mental health professionals we are the instrument from which we do our work. Noticing what arises in you is part of the task. You may read and work through the book for yourself too. Remember, we are our instrument in this work. Our nervous system needs attending to, so we can be an anchor in the storm for our clients. Finding resources to care for yourself is so important. You will find some of those resources in Chapter 6.

SAFETY IS THE BEDROCK

Knowing where to start is key to success. The Felt Sense Polyvagal Model (FSPM) teaches us that creating some sense of safety is the starting point for healing. So, what is safety anyway?

Feelings of safety are not equivalent to objective measurements of safety which could pragmatically be defined as the removal of threat. Feeling safe is more akin to the felt sense described by Eugene Gendlin. Although Gendlin, as a philosopher and psychologist, was not physiologically oriented, he described a "felt sense/shift" as not just a mental experience, but also a physical one. (Winhall & Porges, 2022)

Porges helps us to understand the nature of safety through the lens of the autonomic nervous system. Our top-down culture thinks of safety as the absence of threat. We focus on protecting ourselves by building walls, fences, or security systems, as a way of dealing with physical danger. Our body knows that this is not enough. Our autonomic nervous system requires more than that to feel safe.

Feelings of safety come when we are seen, loved, valued, and when we feel connected and comforted. We feel this when we share a smile, a gentle tone in our voice, a warm embrace. We are social creatures, designed to thrive when we feel safe and held by someone we trust. Sometimes, especially when we don't have access to safe relationships, we feel this connection with our pets and with the natural world. Establishing a sense of connection and belonging in a caring community creates a safe nest in which to grow and heal.

When you feel safe enough the ventral branch of your ANS is activated. Your body feels grounded, and there is a sense of well-being. The ventral branch promotes health, growth, and restoration, the necessary ingredients for healing. In safety we feel clear headed, focused, and present, all characteristics of the most sophisticated part of the brain, the prefrontal cortex. When we feel threatened in states of defense, we lose connection with the ventral branch of the vagus nerve (ventral vagus). Our immune system becomes compromised, making it hard to heal physically and emotionally. This is why it is so important to address safety right from the start.

Many of you reading this book may not be feeling safe enough. Trauma and addiction shift you into states of defense, allowing the trauma feedback loop to prevail. The state of addiction follows this loop over and over, blocking moments of connection because they have been too threatening.

CHANGING DEFINITIONS OF TRAUMA AND SAFETY

Until recently, the traditional Eurocentric definition of trauma has been dominant. This definition sees trauma as a single event that is out of the range of normal experience. A more sophisticated understanding of the nature of trauma is evolving. While the new definition continues to include single traumatic events such as a car accident, there is growing awareness of the need for a separate category that recognizes the impact of being subjected to chronic states of trauma, especially in childhood.

Developmental or *complex trauma*, as it is called, shapes a child's neurophysiological development, putting them at risk for psychological difficulties in adulthood. Systems of oppression such as racism, classism, heteronormativity, poverty, misogyny, and hypermasculinity fuel the underlying causes of trauma and addiction.

Hypermasculinity in particular has contaminated our view of the addicted person. In our top-down Western world we promote a hypermasculine society that idealizes individuality and control. To be addicted in our culture is seen to be dependent, to have lost control. These are qualities associated with femininity, thus relegating the addict to a marginalized group in our society. If you are part of a marginalized group, research shows that you are more at risk for experiencing trauma and addiction (Merrick et al., 2018, p. 1041).

In addition, there are urgent world issues that create a sense of global trauma. The impact of the COVID-19 pandemic and climate change have presented us with tremendously challenging times. At the time of this writing, war has broken out in Ukraine and the Middle East, adding to the increasing levels of conflict. Perhaps more than ever, we are all threatened by stressors that are outside of our day-to-day control. This reality is making it hard to find some sense of calm or optimism about the future. The state of our collective nervous system is often shaky or shutting down in response to the global nature of our traumatic times.

As the definition of trauma broadens it is important to broaden our understanding of safety. Safety in traditional psychological terms is often associated with secure attachment with early caretakers, typically mothers. The majority of research has been done within the context of white middle-class societies where safety has been afforded to many (Dawson, 2018, p. 1). In this context it is thought that most people connect with a sense of safety if they have a caretaker whose autonomic nervous system is ventrally regulated. If they are exposed to threat in a single event, their ANS will shift into flight/fight and return to a ventral state relatively quickly.

However, when we address developmental and global trauma, we appreciate how people are living in chronically traumatic situations. There is no single event, and therefore there is an increasing sense of no return to a safe enough place. Our collective nervous system is struggling to find equanimity.

If you experience safety as illusive, or nonexistent, the word itself can activate the feeling of being unsafe. It can elicit feelings of shame and fear when you can't find a place of safety now, or ever. Or you may have been able to find a time when you felt cozy and safe, but it was quickly destroyed, often repeatedly, by horrible experiences of abuse or neglect. In either case, it can feel quite overwhelming to even say the word *safety*. We see how the nature of what constitutes a felt sense of safety is much more intricate when our definitions change.

CREATIVE WAYS OF FINDING SAFETY

There are many creative ways to find a felt sense of safety. It is important to find what works for you. As we move through the embodied practices you will explore and deepen your own unique felt sense of safety, using different avenues to access the ventral branch of the vagus. Here are some suggestions you can come back to if you want to explore:

A. Replace the word *safety* with *competent*, *capable*, or *able to influence people*. This can bring a sense of confidence which may lead to a sense of grounding or safety. For some people work is a place of feeling capable and seen. Or maybe you enjoy drawing, or sports, or gardening, and you feel content when you are doing these things. This might be a place to start to connect with yourself and your sense of grounding.

B. Find a safe place inside yourself if you cannot find it in your life.

C. Recall feeling a secure attachment to a pet or a person in your community that brings comfort to you, maybe a teacher, friend, or family doctor.

D. Find a spiritual connection with Mother Nature, your ancestors, or God. The Mi'kmaw associate mother, Earth, and the heartbeat of the drum, to evoke feelings of safety and connection. The land becomes a primary source of healing.

Stephen Augustine (n.d.), the Hereditary Chief of the Mi'kmaq Grand Council, described the intimate connection to Mother Earth through the Mi'kmaq Creation Story:

> The third level of creation, down below us, is our Mother Earth, on whom we walk and who bears the spirits of our ancestors. The interconnective relationship between Mother Earth and the whole of creation is evident in the Mi'kmaw language. The Mi'kmaw words for the people, and for the Earth, and for mother, and the drum, all come from that term which refers to "the surface on which we stand, and which we share with other surface dwellers." And so, when we talk about the drum, we are talking about our Mother the Earth. When we hear that drumbeat, we are hearing the heartbeat of our Mother the Earth. And so, it is understood that when we drum, we are acknowledging that we are children of the Earth and that we are sending a message back to our own mother, saying, "we hear you, we understand, and we recognize your heartbeat in the same way that a child after it is born recognizes the heartbeat of its own mother." (Tipple, 2021, p. 1)

E. **Find moment-by-moment safety.** This happens when you find a fleeting moment that feels okay. Allow yourself to slow down your pace and take a little deeper breath. As you slow down, a quiet space can form, an opening that brings you into the present moment. When you do this, you can begin to acknowledge that right here and now, as far as you know, you are safe enough. *In fact, all we really ever have is moment-by-moment safety.* We have no idea what the next second of our lives will bring us. Most of the time we use some form of dissociation to protect us from recognizing this. When a crisis occurs, it reminds us how fragile our existence really is. Facing this helps to acknowledge how vulnerable we are, and at the same time, to offer a moment-by-moment sense of grounding in present awareness. Learning to welcome this awareness of our vulnerability is part of body wisdom. We are what Gendlin calls "shaky beings" (Gendlin, 1990).

F. Another way of thinking about safety and grounding comes from having a purpose. The famous Holocaust survivor Viktor Frankl wrote "Life is never made unbearable by circumstances, but only by lack of meaning and purpose" (1984). Trauma often shatters one's sense of meaning or purpose in life. Finding your way back to something that you care about and believe in is risky business. You have been disappointed so many times. But it is essential in being able to heal. Hope is necessary to find meaning and purpose. Without hope, what is the point? Without hope you cannot imagine a future that is full of the ventral energy of aliveness.

Finding your way back to your body releases stuck patterns of hopelessness. What gives you a sense of purpose? What do you believe in? Take a breath, say hello to your body. Let your body know that you are on your way back to it. You will be surprised at how this embodied connection will promote your health, your growth, and the restoration of your life. The life that you so dearly deserve. Many survivors of trauma find meaning in helping others. There is a profound sense of purpose in being part of a community that works toward alleviating suffering.

G. Use your imagination to construct a safe place. Some people do this through fantasizing, drawing, writing, dancing. As it becomes clearer you can cultivate a felt sense of safety from your own creative process.

Now it's time to pause, take a breath, and directly experience your start on this path.

This *pausing* activity may be unfamiliar and uncomfortable for you. Pausing connects you to yourself, to your bodily awareness, and subsequently to others. Numbing or dissociating as it is called, blocks this bodily awareness to protect you from perceived threat. Your healing journey will help you to reduce threat. And as you reduce threat, your body will seek connection. Bodies crave warmth and love. You cannot heal alone. Connection with others who are safe is the key to healing.

PREPARING: INTENTION AND HOPE

Like many things in life, learning to plan ahead is key to achieving what you want. This is very challenging to do when you are living in a traumatized state. Trauma locks us in the past, while preparing is dependent upon imagining the future. Bringing attention to your purpose, your deep desire, and perhaps urgent need to help yourself is a necessary step in the beginning. Along the way you will need to remind yourself of the importance of being intentional. That's because it is hard to let go of soothing habits and behaviors that work very effectively to help you manage the unmanageable. Until they don't! As you develop these daily practices your capacity to be intentional about your life will grow.

Healing requires some sense of hope and good energy that you can bring to the work, otherwise you become debilitated. So, it is very important to intentionally look for something helpful to accompany you. Maybe someone has inspired you to set an intention to heal. Watching other people who seem to be living a good life is a very helpful way to begin. We can learn so much from others. Look for examples of ways that you see people managing their lives, the choices that they make, and how their paths lead to success in reaching their goals. Sometimes hope lies in the strength of communities. People pulling together to heal global trauma.

If it's hard for you to find hope, you can borrow some of mine to get you started. Bodies are like that. They are highly attuned to how others feel. Have you noticed that sometimes, not all the time, you can start to feel better when you are with someone who is feeling good? My hope comes from what I have learned over 40 years of being a trauma/addiction therapist. During that time, I discovered new ways of healing that are different and have proved to be more effective than the traditional models of treatment. These new ways work with *body wisdom*. While they have been around in other cultures, they are new to the Western world view. The Felt Sense Polyvagal Model (FSPM) helps you to heal by teaching you the skills to access body wisdom.

The first three practices are designed to help you prepare, to create enough of a safe nest so that you have the necessary ingredients to begin. Creating a good foundation provides you with the sense of safety in knowing that you have something to fall back on. As you go through each practice ask yourself if you have what you need. Are you safe enough to start this journey?

*Practice 1. The Five P's

The Five P's are: **place** and time; **pacing**; **pausing** and triggers; **partnership**; and **presence**. Together these help provide a solid foundation to begin your journey.

Place and Time

Create a private uninterrupted space and regular time(s) each week, preferably one hour per week to start. Eventually you will begin a daily practice.

Finding your own quiet, private space, and a regular time is often very challenging when you are struggling. It requires a lot of commitment on your part. If you are having trouble, ask yourself, "What is getting in the way of finding a private space, and/or a regular weekly time?"

Often space is limited in your home, and it requires going out to find a quiet place. Sometimes finding a corner in a coffee shop, a park, or a library is the only way at the beginning. Sometimes people find it hard to feel entitled to a private, uninterrupted space at home. Making yourself a priority can feel impossible when you have put others ahead of yourself in order to feel safe and loved. Practicing making boundaries with family is an important step. Try saying "I need an hour of uninterrupted time to myself, so I will see you later." You may find that it feels scary to ask for this. This is part of the journey in making your well-being a priority. Remember that when you take care of yourself, you are also taking care of the people who need you.

If you get stuck here, that is understandable. Many people do. It means that it's time to see a therapist to help you take the first, essential step.

Pacing

This journey is usually slow, and often challenging. Knowing this helps you to be more patient with yourself. Slow and steady is a good rhythm to aim for. It takes time for bodies to change. If you get overwhelmed, you can stop reading and stay with grounding practices for as long as you need to.

Sometimes people feel very excited and hopeful at the beginning of a new endeavor, like making a New Year's resolution. You feel lots of energy and attention to the practices, particularly if you have others supporting you. You may experience deep felt shifts in your body, easing your fears, and giving you a lot of encouragement. Savor this.

As time goes on, many folks find the journey becomes more challenging as they engage in practices that involve working with traumatic feelings. This is totally understandable, even predictable. Here is a place to remind yourself to pace. You need to honor your body's need to slow down and rewire.

Pausing and Triggers

Triggers, moments of acute discomfort and dysregulation of your ANS, are part of the healing journey. This is natural because we are, as gently as possible, venturing into the part of your life that has caused you to retreat. Triggers distort present moment experiences when past traumas come alive, crashing into your current life in a powerful and disturbing way. Reframing how you view triggers can be a very helpful way of attending to yourself at these times. Instead of pushing them away, you can view triggers as wounded places, lost parts of yourself, longing to be heard, to be honored and to be healed. It becomes easier to manage triggers as you develop your skills in the practices. Once you learn how to get some distance from the triggers, then you can be with them without becoming them.

We will be working with triggers later in the book, but for now it is important to point out that often people do fall back into the trauma feedback loop along the way. The body goes back to what it knows from the past when it is activated. You find yourself numbing, engaging in old bad habits and addictions. If you have support from family or friends, you may be ashamed to tell them how you are doing.

It is common to want to give up. So here especially, remember to come back to Chapter 1 to refresh. You have not lost all that you gained. *You just need to regroup!* The work that you have already done in the book is still there in front of you. The neuropathways of healing have not been destroyed. They are there, waiting to be reawakened. It's just that bodies have ways of protecting us, and you have to work with your body to update your autonomic nervous system.

You are not lazy, unmotivated, undeserving, or hopeless. Your body is simply doing what it knows how to do to protect you when it feels unsafe. So, befriend your body, knowing that when you get triggered the "not so smart" part of your brain takes over. Like your dog, it wants to protect you, and doesn't always read the situation well. You have to train your dog, and you have to train your frightened nervous system.

If you feel consistently triggered, your body is letting you know that it doesn't feel safe enough to engage with the process. It's important to discuss this with a therapist for more support. You may be in a physically unsafe situation, and your body is telling you that it needs more safety to shift ANS states.

Partnership

The most important thing to do now is to find a FSPM partner that can accompany you. It may be me at the very beginning, but as you move into Chapter 2 you will need to find a therapist, body worker, coach, and/or someone who is willing to work through the prac-

tices with you. As you meet with your partner you can take turns reading the practices to each other and/or have a Focusing session (more on this in Chapter 3).

Trauma and addiction result in isolation. The way that isolation shows up is in the unrelenting ache of loneliness. Remember that when you are stuck in the trauma feedback loop, limited ventral energy is available. Your social engagement system, the part of you that seeks connection with others, is dulled, protecting you from perceived threat. While you may feel lonely, you avoid reaching out to others. Reaching for that thing, or that way of being that soothes you, feels right at the time. But it keeps you stuck in the unrelenting ache of loneliness.

Connecting with others is key in your healing journey. The ventral branch of your ANS activates when you connect with others, shifting you out of the trauma feedback loop and into health, growth, and restoration. It also builds in accountability. Your partner and/or therapist helps you to stay intentional and accountable to yourself.

A word about accountability. The FSPM teaches you to be able to do two important things that may seem contradictory. You approach your journey with kindness and a deep understanding of your body's reverting back to trauma behaviors to survive. At the same time, you hold yourself accountable to being honest and vulnerable in self reporting your progress. The more you understand how your ANS works to keep you alive, the more you heal your shame. This makes it much easier to be honest about your trauma responses.

It is understandable and common for trauma survivors to lie as a way of coping. You may have learned that hiding the truth protects you from an abuser, and/or allows you to continue with addictive behaviors. Or maybe you find yourself dissociating and not remembering things. Perhaps others notice this and ask you about it. You freeze, not knowing how to answer, so you lie. You may be surprised to know that lying is a very common survival strategy. I have grown to expect that folks will lie out of necessity in situations that feel threatening. So again, it is understandable.

But now, you need to allow yourself to be vulnerable in honoring your truth with your therapist/FSPM partner. When you hold yourself accountable, with the support of your partner, you begin the process of documenting your embodied journey. It's very important to know if your body feels ready to shift states. If you are struggling it means that you must listen to your body and adjust accordingly.

Let's pause here and ask yourself, "Have I lied to myself and/or the people around me to cover up for behaving in ways that I am ashamed of or don't understand? Am I ready to hold myself accountable and commit to the truth?"

Presence

The 20 embodied practices guide you in developing presence. Western culture likes to move fast, searching for the shiny new thing. Embodied change requires slowing down and repeating embodied practices. This allows you to become more present in the moment. Each practice builds healing neuropathways. At first it may feel very new and different to slow down, and to go over practices that you have already completed.

Remember, you are shifting paradigms. In this new way of being more connected to your body, you slow down and realize that every time you bring your attention down into your body, it is fresh and new. Moment by moment experiencing is always new. While the practice may be the same, the process is always fresh because we have never been in this moment before. As you pause, you invite something new to come. It takes patience, and the ability to pause and notice . . . pause and notice . . . pause and notice . . .

As you practice you become more and more present to your life. While this can be scary at first, finding this deep connection with aliveness slowly becomes a source of comfort and even joy. You can develop a secure attachment to yourself. This means you learn to trust yourself, to soothe and calm that part of you that is upset. You become your own best friend.

Gather Materials

Gather all the downloads at janwinhall.com, including Body Cards, FSPM 7 F states model and Four Circles handouts, Practice Recording forms (free downloads), crayons (for the Body Cards), a journal, and/or drawing paper. You will need a secure place to keep all your materials.

Many people find that they are concerned about keeping a journal or other materials because someone may find them. Keeping your notes on your computer can be helpful. You can take pictures of your Body Cards and store them on your computer. You can also purchase a briefcase that can be locked. It is very important that you have a secure spot to keep your documents so that you feel safe to be really honest with yourself.

Now it's time to begin Practice 2 (Noticing the Space Around You) where we will slow down and make a quiet space inside.

*Practice 2. Noticing the Space Around You

Sitting or standing in the private place where you will be using this book, begin to slow down and allow yourself to notice the space around you. What do you see, feel, hear, smell? What are you drawn back to in the room? It's important to have something in the room that anchors you into a feeling of grounding or safety. (If you don't see anything, find something that you can bring into your space.) Bring your attention to something pleasurable to look at, to touch, to hold. Practice being able to stay here for several minutes. If it is hard at first, you can try counting softly to yourself. . . . Count to 60 and start again three times.

With practice this will awaken a calm place in the body, a beginning safe space. You will see as we move through the material that healing is very much about what you learn to pay attention to. You will return to this practice as a resource when you need to settle your body.

*Practice 3. The Pause

Start your practice by noticing what is around you. Take your time with the space that you have created. Feel your feet on the floor, soften your gaze. Notice if it feels safe to close your eyes. If not, you could bring attention to an object in the room that helps calm you. Now ask into your body, "How am I feeling about beginning this healing journey with Jan?" Notice where you feel a sensation in your body. Place a hand gently on this part of your body. Can you find a word, image, sound, or gesture, that describes this sensation? If nothing comes, that is just fine. Your body will speak to you when it feels safe enough.

Now gently return to Practice 2, Noticing the Space Around You.

Bring your attention to something pleasurable to look at, to touch, to hold. This will awaken a calm place in the body—a beginning safe space.

SUMMARY

In this chapter we have begun to build the necessary ingredients to help you create a safe enough nest in which to do this work. We explored different ways of understanding and defining safety and trauma. You have practiced the Five P's that lay the foundation for healing:

P*lace and Time*
P*acing*
P*ausing and Triggers*
P*artnership*
P*resence*

Now that you have read through this chapter, consider whether you feel ready to continue to Chapter 2. Ask yourself, "Do I feel ready to go on or is there still work to be done with the Five P's? Would I like to stay with Practices 2 and 3?" There is no rush, and it is wise to take your time. And of course, you will come back to these practices, time and again, as we continue on. Repetition is a resource.

Finding Safety in the Body: The Felt Sense Polyvagal Model (Practices 4–5)

Now you are here in your quiet, private space. You have managed to carve out an hour to be with yourself. (If an hour feels impossible, break it down to 30-minute intervals, increasing it by 5 minutes at a time.) You have completed your preparation and are ready to go on. That is quite an accomplishment! It is really important to acknowledge your progress. You don't have to be afraid to celebrate because even if you struggle, you have not lost all you gained. Your new neuropathways are still there. Take a breath and let yourself feel into the good ventral energy of progress.

Chapter 2 presents the Felt Sense Polyvagal Model in the graphic form. You will learn more about the autonomic nervous system and the five lessons in Polyvagal Theory. This will help you to understand how you came to be where you are and how to shift paths. But before we dig into this, let's start by slowing things down and inviting a quiet moment. We start by returning to the pause, so you can begin to connect with body wisdom. Remember, *repetition is a resource.*

Practice 2. Noticing the Space Around You (from Chapter 1)

Sitting or standing in the private place where you will be using this book, begin to slow down and allow yourself to notice the space around you. What do you see, feel, hear, smell? What are you drawn back to in the room? It's important to have something in the room that anchors you into a feeling of grounding or safety. (If you don't see anything, find something that you can bring into your space.) Bring your attention to something pleasurable to look at, to touch, to hold. Practice being able to stay here for several minutes. If it is hard at first, you can try counting softly to yourself. . . . Count to 60 and start again three times.

With practice this will awaken a calm place in the body, a beginning safe space. You will see as we move through the material that healing is very much about what you learn to pay attention to. You will return to this practice as a resource when you need to settle your body.

THE TRADITIONAL ANS

To appreciate Polyvagal Theory, it is helpful to know how the autonomic nervous system was understood before Dr. Porges's research. The traditional model of the ANS was seen as having two opposing subsystems: the ventral parasympathetic state that allows us to rest and digest, and the sympathetic state that activates us into a flight/fight state when we feel threatened. Porges says, "We were all taught that the sympathetic state meant stress, and was always bad, while the parasympathetic state meant relaxation, and was always good" (Porges, 2023, p. 57). He goes on to describe how the two states were seen as antagonistic, stuck in an "eternal battle for our bodies" (p. 57).

PORGES'S PARADOX

Early on in his career Porges began researching heart rate patterns in newborn babies. He assumed that the ventral parasympathetic vagus, the "good" vagus, would act as a protective feature that could help predict positive outcomes for newborns. After publishing a paper on the subject in 1992 in the journal *Pediatrics* he received a letter from a neonatologist. This fellow challenged the traditional view, suggesting that the ventral vagus was *not* protective, but that it could in fact kill us.

A light bulb moment occurred for Dr. Porges as he read this letter and reflected on his experience. One would assume given the traditional view of the ANS that babies under stress would be experiencing activation of the sympathetic flight/fight response, with increased heart rate. The letter pointed to the fact that premature babies in distress were experiencing bradycardia. This is a slowing of the heart rate, that in some babies resulted in death. This slowing of heart rate was puzzling because it is the opposite of what researchers expected.

For several months Porges carried this letter around in his briefcase. He asked himself how it could be that the ventral vagus, which is supposed to promote health, could also be responsible for causing death? This paradox intrigued him, and his curious and open nature led him to pursue the resolution of the vagal paradox.

PORGES'S POLYVAGAL INFORMED ANS: ANCIENT DORSAL VAGUS AND MODERN VENTRAL VAGUS

As he continued with his research, Porges observed that the vagus nerve is made up of multiple discrete motor branches. One branch, called the *ventral vagus*, slows us down, helping us to heal. Another branch also slows us down but could be life threatening if it causes bradycardia. Porges named this branch the *dorsal vagus*. Understanding that there are two vagal branches solved the paradox, but how and when did the dorsal branch become activated?

Porges answered these questions by studying the changes that occurred in the neural regulation of the ANS through evolution. Our reptilian ancestors have an ancient vagus nerve that is unmyelinated and responds to threat with bradycardia and shutting down by "playing dead."

The ventral vagus appears more recently in modern mammals, including humans. This branch is myelinated, meaning it is contained in a fatty sheath that accelerates the efficiency of the vagus to help promote healing. The process of myelination occurs in the later months of pregnancy.

Now the response of the babies in the neonatal unit made sense. Because they were premature their little nervous systems didn't have a developed ventral vagus that had the benefit of myelination. So, their dorsal vagus was in charge, and they were shutting down in order to survive.

INTRODUCING THE FELT SENSE POLYVAGAL MODEL GRAPHIC: A BODY FRIENDLY TOOL

A graphic version of the Felt Sense Polyvagal Model (FSPM), including both client and clinician examples, was created with the help of many clients, therapists, and students over several decades. We simplified the client model by using words

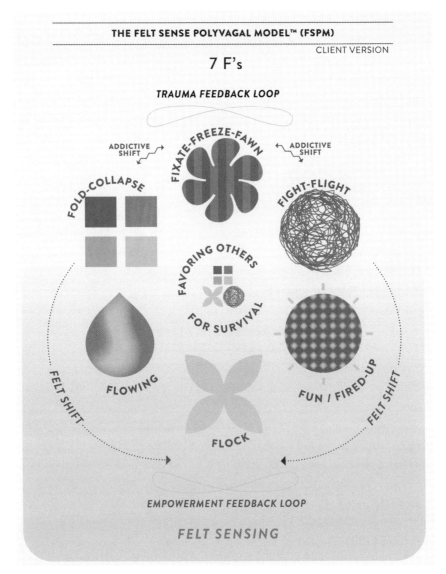

Figure 2.1: The Felt Sense Polyvagal Model™ (FSPM) Client Version, 7 F's
Source: Copyright © 2021 From *Treating Trauma and Addiction with the Felt Sense Polyvagal Model: A Bottom-Up Approach*, Jan Winhall. Reproduced by permission of Taylor and Francis Group, LLC, a division of Informa plc.

that begin with the letter *F* to name the states of the autonomic nervous system (see Figure 2.1). Graphic images resonate with our bodily experience. They involve bottom-up processing by engaging the right hemisphere of the brain. This part of our brain is involved in the two key processes of the FSPM, interoception and neuroception. The right hemisphere is responsible for creative, nonlinear, big picture thinking. It is where dreams are made and where the felt sense is formed. The graphic models are designed to activate embodied right hemisphere processing with the use of playful imagery. Circles activate nonlinear thinking, hence the only place where boxes appear (linear, top-down processing) is in the dorsal state of shutting down and disconnection. Color images evoke emotional responses, activating the felt sense of interoceptive awareness. Learning about your ANS through the use of imagery and color is "body friendly." This process engages the ventral vagus, creating a playful embodied container, a safe nest in which to do your healing.

See insert after p. 128 for color figure.

DESCRIPTION OF THE 7 F STATES

The autonomic nervous system has three main states (Flock, Fight/Flight, Fold) and four blended states (Fun/Fired Up, Fixate/Freeze/Fawn, Flowing, and Favoring Others for Survival) made up of combinations of the three main states.

The client version of the FSPM uses imagery and color to describe three main states: Flock (yellow, ventral), Fight/Flight (red, sympathetic), and Fold (gray, dorsal).

We will first deal with the three main states.

1. Flock—(Yellow) Ventral State of Safety, Social Engagement, and Felt Sensing

This state promotes health, growth, and restoration. The ventral state fosters compassion, creativity, community, connection. Ventral energy must be present for a felt sense to fully form. In this state the body shape is composed of the following: alert mind, relaxed body, open, curious, friendly, regular heart rate. The deepening of the yellow color in the bottom half of the model depicts the intensity of ventral energy, hence the intensity of a fully formed felt sense.

2. Fight/Flight—(Red) Sympathetic State

In this state, we feel threatened and the body mobilizes to protect us. Also in this state, our immune system is compromised.

Fight is a mobilizing state of anger/rage. Our body shape is: constricted limbs, clenched jaw and hands, mobilized to attack. We are hyperfocused on the threat with increased heart rate and accelerated breathing.

Flight is a state of fear and anxiety. In this state, the body mobilizes to run and escape. Here the body shape is: constricted limbs, increased heart rate, scanning for danger, pupils dilated, increased perspiration, flushed cheeks, poised to run.

3. Fold—(Gray) Dorsal Response

Fold is a collapse of the ANS into a dissociative state when the sympathetic response is ineffective. In this state we feel deep sadness, depression, or absence of feeling, and our immune system is compromised. Our body shape is: slumped, folded inward, with heavy, numbed limbs, vacant eyes, and exhaustion.

Pause here and familiarize yourself with the three main states in the autonomic nervous system by looking at the model. Let your body appreciate the colors and shapes. Trace the pathways and notice the trauma feedback loop. What are you drawn to?

FOUR BLENDED STATES OF THE ANS

The autonomic nervous system is also capable of blending the three main states, allowing the body to respond with a variety of options. As we are studying the ANS more blended states are being discussed and included in the Polyvagal Theory. They are:

4. Fun or Fired Up—(Red, Yellow) Ventral/Sympathetic

This is a blending of Flock and Flight/Fight, an excited state. You feel grounded in ventral with some sympathetic. This may feel like a solid connection with your feet, along with some increase in heart rate and a bit of tightness and/or goosebumps.

5. Fixate/Freeze/Fawn—(Red, Gray)

This is a blending of states that shifts you back and forth from Flight/Fight to Fold. These are the states involved in the **Trauma Feedback Loop**. Here you feel tightness, collapse, and numbing. This state often uses addictions to try to regulate. Being caught up in this feedback loop feels very unregulated. Your moods are swinging back and forth to try to cope with overwhelming, painful, scary feelings. Ventral energy is not present. This is also the same blending of states involved in Fawning, a dissociated state where you are complying with a bully and hiding yourself to survive.

6. Favoring Others for Survival—(Yellow, Red, Gray) Ventral, Sympathetic, Dorsal

This state is a blending of all three main nervous system states, Flock, Flight/Fight, and Fold. You may experience your body moving through constriction, and then some numbing, and also having a sense of grounding and connection. This feels like you move in and out of feeling present. The body is cycling through all three states, some tightness, some numbing, and with varying degrees of grounded connection with your sense of "self" and your need to protect yourself in that moment. You feel your feet on the ground when ventral energy is intermittently available to you.

7. Flowing—(Gray, Yellow) Dorsal/Ventral

This is a grounded, peaceful state, with the safety of Flock, and the stillness of Fold. It is a sweet spot where the body feels calm and nourished. Relaxed muscles, regular heartbeat, and resting deeply into a state of surrender. A place of meditation, Focusing, prayer, and intimacy.

This next practice helps you recognize and connect with the seven autonomic states of the FSPM. This practice is the first step in developing the FSPM skill of Recognizing/Retuning the autonomic nervous system. It invites you to become familiar with the bodily sensations of each state through connecting with muscle tone, breath, feelings, and sensations. First we begin with the three main states. We start with recognizing what ANS state you are currently in, because healing starts with understanding how safe you feel in your body.

*Practice 4. Recognizing/Retuning Your Nervous System States: The 7 F States

Sitting or standing in your private space, allow yourself to arrive. Start by noticing the space around you. See if you can pause and pay attention to one thing in the room. If it feels right for you, soften your gaze. Take your time here, and then check to see if it would be alright to close your eyes. If not, you can also choose to keep your eyes open. With time it will become easier to feel yourself drop down inside your body.

Feel your feet on the floor and slowly turn your attention inwards, down into the center of your body. Say a friendly hello to your inside self. As you experience your body from the inside, notice how you are holding yourself. How is your body carrying you? Notice your muscles, your breath, your limbs. First, we start with the three main states: Fight/ Flight, Flock, and Fold.

Are you held tight, anxious, and wound up in a sympathetic state? Are you feeling frustrated and angry in Fight; or worried and scared in Flight?

Or maybe your muscles are loose, comfortable, and your breathing is relaxed in a ventral state. You feel friendly and grounded in Flock.

Perhaps your muscles are heavy, and your body feels lethargic, in a dorsal state. Your mood is sad, depressed, or numb and is disconnected in Fold.

Pause here. Take your time to try on these different states. Our bodies know each state, as they are designed to shift us without our conscious awareness. Over time you may discover that you have a default state or pathway that your body has become habituated to.

Now we explore the blended states.

Fun/Fired Up feels grounded with a bit of excitement, like when you are playing, or feeling passionate about life.

Fixate/Freeze/Fawn feels stuck, oscillating back and forth from anxiety to numbing. Often bad habits, obsessing, and addictions are present. The body is struggling to move, spinning around in a dead-end cycle. You can feel a mixture of excitement, anxiety, depression, isolation, and deadness.

Favoring Others for Survival is a state of hyperarousal, on guard to appease the people who have power and control over you. Survival is based on helping others at the expense of your own needs. Marginalized groups in our society often live in this state.

Over the next days allow yourself to come back here and notice how your body feels. You will begin to recognize your different states as your body speaks to you. No one state is better than the other. While we feel good in a ventral state, we need the others to help us when we don't feel safe enough to be fully present. As you begin an inner dialogue with your body about safety you can assess what needs to happen in your life to bring more flock energy. Later, in Practice 12 (Four Circle Harm Reduction Practice), we will document your specific activities that help you build ventral pathways.

THE GRAPHIC MODEL AS A VISUAL ROADMAP

As you reflect on the different states, many of you may resonate with the trauma feedback loop as your current path. It is normal to feel very lost here, so having a map that helps you to see where you are and where you need to go is essential. It's sad and can be painful to see so clearly how you are missing out on the yellow ventral pathway of felt sensing. No wonder you are struggling! The good news is that now you can begin to understand how you got here, and how you can change. That is empowering.

The FSPM is a body friendly map that invites your felt sense to become curious. It gently awakens your feelings, your senses, your connection to awareness of something lost, and something found. The graphic model becomes a visual cue for safety as you begin to see where you are in your nervous system, how you got there, and what you need to do to shift into a more ventral pathway that brings health, growth, and restoration.

As you become more familiar with the 7 F states you will learn how to trace your journey. This awakens lost neuropathways that facilitate a deeper connection with the parts of yourself you have buried. While this can be frightening at first, it is an important step in the journey toward healing. As you perform the practices you will be moving through your untold story, weaving in your embodied journey through the 7 F states, and reclaiming your body's capacity to a felt sense that will provide liberation from the endless loop of trauma and addiction.

CLINICIAN FSPM

Starting with the client version helps to make the model simple. It enables practitioners to teach complex top-down polyvagal concepts while simultaneously engaging bottom-up felt sensing. By targeting both, embodied learning is profoundly impactful. Once the client version has been used for a while, some people enjoy looking at the more complex clinician version (see Figure 2.2). For example, in Chapter 5, we will be doing a practice that takes you into rela-

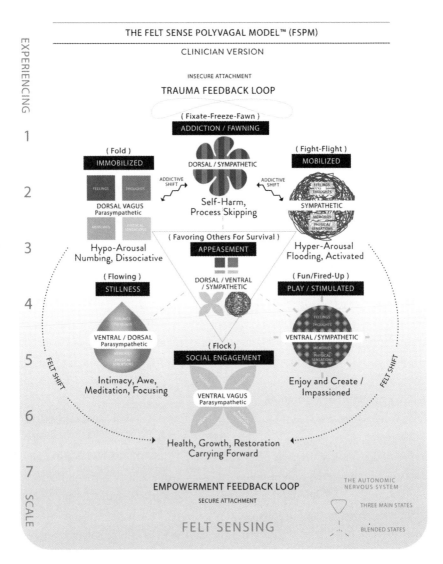

Figure 2.2: The Felt Sense Polyvagal Model™ (FSPM) Clinician Version
Source: Copyright © 2021 From *Treating Trauma and Addiction with the Felt Sense Polyvagal Model: A Bottom-Up Approach*, Jan Winhall. Reproduced by permission of Taylor and Francis Group, LLC, a division of Informa plc.

tionships with early caregivers. The clinician model incorporates concepts like secure and insecure attachment styles.

See insert after p. 128 for color figure.

FIVE LESSONS IN POLYVAGAL THEORY

These are foundational principles of the polyvagal approach.

1. Safety First: Safety is the Bedrock, None of Us Are Safe Unless All of Us Are Safe

By now you are aware of how safety is the organizing principal in Polyvagal Theory, and in trauma and addiction treatment. Our most grounded, compassionate, and wise self shows up in safety. Addictions don't occur when we feel safe enough. These are two very good reasons to make safety our North Star.

> The capacity to ground ourselves, to feel safe and regulated inside our bodies, is the most fundamental skill we can achieve in a lifetime. Some of us learn these skills and the felt sense in our bodies from our loving caretakers. Some have this capacity early on in life but lose it with experiences of pain and suffering. Others spend the better part of their existence trying to create this safe nest in which to grow and heal. (Winhall, 2021, p. 116)

Let's take some time here to assess where you are in the above quote. Did you start off in a safe nest with your parents/caretakers? How much do you know about their history? What was the context in which they grew up? Were they struggling with trauma and addiction?

Is your family impacted by systems of oppression? Intergenerational trauma lives in our bodies. It's important to learn more about your family history if you can. Let yourself journey back to explore your parents' lives, and their parents' lives. If you don't know about your family history, you can invite your body to be curious about your roots. Many times, we don't have facts about our trauma, but we do have body memories that we can become more aware of.

If you were fortunate enough to have started life with enough safety, you will have that imprinted in your body. The ventral pathway will be formed and receptive to your nurturance. Do you have a sense of what ruptured your feeling of safety? How old were you? Were other people aware that you felt unsafe?

If you did not have a safe enough start, did you find a harbor along the way? Some relationship that felt connected? Some people find a neighbor that took them in. Sometimes grandparents create a cozy space. Some people flourish at school and feel a kind of confidence and safety from that experience. This is a good place to take some time to make notes, perhaps discuss with your family members and/or friends who may have known you as a child.

In addition to our own unique experiences, we must recognize that we all are citizens of the world, all interconnected and dependent on each other for safety. Polyvagal Theory reminds us that no one is safe unless we are all safe enough. The COVID-19 pandemic made this very clear. Healing from global trauma is a community effort. Our collective awareness of suffering challenges us to do more to help. It is not only a compassionate act, but it also makes sense when we understand that through a polyvagal lens, we are wired to create safety for each other in order to survive and thrive.

2. Interoception: Honor Your Mind/Body Connection

In the Western world we aspire to be like sophisticated, smooth-running machines. We value our cognitive abilities over the messiness of feelings or bodily awareness. This is reflected in our preference for top-down approaches, the so called "hard sciences." This results in a favoring of cognitive behavioral therapy to address the emotional turmoil that increasing numbers of people are experiencing. More recently, we are seeing a movement in the treatment of trauma toward honoring body wisdom. Polyvagal Theory is at the forefront of this paradigm shift, providing an evidence-based approach that is both top down and bottom up.

Interoception, the process by which we sense into our bodily knowing, is an important part of Polyvagal Theory because it helps us to appreciate the bidirectionality of information that is carried by the vagus nerve to the brain stem. In fact, 80% of that information is afferent, meaning that it moves from the body to the brain, from the bottom up (Porges, 2023). As you hone your skills in befriending your body you are connecting with interoception.

Focusing is our body's natural process of interoception. It helps us to become deeply aware of the pathway from mind to body, and body to mind. Like yoga, dance, drumming, or chanting, Focusing taps into our sense of connection with our whole embodied self. When we feel integrated, we are connected to the ventral energy of grounding. Because the trauma feedback loop cuts us off from bodily knowing, these interoceptive practices form the basis of the 20 embodied practices in the FSPM.

Polyvagal Theory teaches us that it is time for the Western world to stop turning its back on the body. Embracing body wisdom is a polyvagal truth. In Chapter 3 we will take a deep dive into the interoceptive practice of felt sensing.

3. Neuroception: Our Body's Wisdom is Designed to Seek Safety

Neuroception, our unconscious safety monitor, is foundational. Our body seeks safety and survival by shifting nervous system states to adapt to our environment. By now you are becoming familiar with the concept of neuroception. Rather than *describing* it, we are going to engage the body in helping us to *experience* it. While the process is unconscious, we can engage the awareness of neuroception through tapping into interoception, the felt sense of it.

Porges states, "Although we are usually not aware of the cues that trigger neuroception, we tend to be aware of the physiological shift (i.e., interoception). Sometimes we experience this shift as feelings in our gut or heart or as an intuition that the context is dangerous" (Porges, 2023, p. 198).

Gendlin saw this physiological shift and initially called it a "moment of movement." Later he formally named it the felt shift. "Direct reference, (to felt sense) as well as the resulting symbolizations, involves bodily felt tension relief" (1986, p. 13).

*Practice 5. The Felt Sense of Neuroception

I invite you now to take some time to slow down, feeling into the present moment. Notice the space around you. Allow yourself to pause. Check to see if now is a good time to go inside and explore your body's response to the concept of neuroception. Soften your gaze and see if you can begin to find a pathway into your body's knowing. In the same way that your body knows how to adjust your temperature, your body knows how to read a situation and adjust your nervous system to protect you. Let yourself really appreciate and honor how your body is designed to take care of you. You have an inner compass. You just have to feel safe enough to be able to listen for it.

Imagine that your neuroceptive process, your Inner Guide to safety, is an animal, or a favorite person, or a spiritual presence. Let yourself get to know this presence in whatever form it comes to you. What does it look like, what sounds does it make, how does it sit in your body? See if you can place your hands where you feel it in your body. Does this Inner Guide to safety have a name? Take some time to be with this felt sense. Explore your thoughts, feelings, physical sensations, and memories. You may want to journal or draw your experience.

Faulty Neuroception: What Helped You Now Harms You

Remember, while it is true that we can draw strength from the wisdom of the body, it is also true that the trauma feedback loop creates faulty neuroception when we get triggered. We think we are in danger when we are not. Often trauma survivors feel betrayed by their bodies because of this. It feels like your body is misleading you and creating a lot of havoc in your life.

Here is the important thing to realize. Neuroception is based on information coming from the brain stem. This is the least sophisticated part of your brain. It isn't concerned with nuance. It is concerned with survival. We don't have time to think and plan and examine ideas when we are under threat. Much like your dog, actions in response to neuroception are based on instinct. If you are in real danger, hesitation can get you killed on the spot. But with faulty neuroception, we become triggered. Then we feel like we are in danger when we aren't. If you work with your neuroception, be kind to yourself like you are with your dog, it will begin to rewire. It is hopeful to realize that each time you do these practices you are healing. As this process develops, you will be able to observe events that would have triggered you in the past, but now seem less and less intense. Your capacity to stay grounded increases and you feel more solid, more confident, more connected to others, more alive. This is a truly marvelous feeling. It takes time, and it does happen.

Necessity is the Mother of Invention

It's interesting to note that both Gendlin and Porges invented new terms for embodied processes: Gendlin's "Focusing and felt sense" and Porges's "neuroception." The need for new words reflects the top-down nature of Western culture. There simply were no words for these bottom-up processes because they were not recognized. Giving language to them promotes the development of somatic knowledge, enabling us to advocate for a new paradigm. We harness the wisdom of the body by naming and describing the way that it functions, and the gifts that it brings to us. We appreciate the way that each of these embodied processes aids in our survival and our ability to thrive in life.

4. Social Engagement: We Need Each Other to Feel Safe and Connected, and to Heal

We have discussed the evolutionary timeline in the development of the ANS. The dorsal branch is the oldest, originating 500 million years ago. The sympathetic nervous system evolved 400 million years ago. The newest, uniquely mammalian ventral vagal pathway developed 200 million years ago. As mammals, we developed as social beings. We thrive when we feel close to others.

Flock, as we call this ventral pathway in the FSPM, is the home of what Porges calls the social engagement system (Porges, 2023). The social engagement system involves brain stem areas that regulate the ventral vagus and also regulate the muscles of the face, head, eyes, ears, and voice. This branch of the vagus communicates with the areas above the diaphragm. It forms bidirectional communication between our face and heart. Through this process we encourage people to connect with us by smiling and giving cues of safety, or we signal the need for distance by frowning or looking away. Our tone of voice and degree of eye contact indicate whether we are friendly. Through neuroception we determine how socially engaged those around us are and how engaged we want to be.

Polyvagal Theory views social engagement as a biological imperative, meaning that we need connection to survive. Through connection with the ventral vagus, the home of the social engagement system, our physiology is coregulated to optimize mental and physical health. Therefore, the need for activation of the social engagement system cannot be stressed enough. This is why we work so often in partnerships and groups. Connection is the cure for healing trauma and addiction.

Social Engagement and the Trauma Feedback Loop: Diverging Agendas

We are wired to Flock together in good times and bad. When we feel safe, we are motivated to reach out to others, to connect and develop lasting relationships. We experience this unique connection with other animals, particularly mammals, forming strong social bonds with our pets. For trauma survivors these can be our easiest, most trusted friends.

When we are living in the trauma feedback loop, we lose access to the ventral vagus, hence we lose access to our social engagement system. In the dysregulated states of flight/fight, fixate/fawn, and fold/collapse, we give and receive cues of threat and shutdown, avoiding eye contact and warding off others attempts to be close to us. Because we have been so hurt, our body's agenda is to seek protection. This may be the very state that you are experiencing in your life now. As we saw in the graphic model, the problem with the trauma feedback loop is that you are missing out on all the good stuff in life, the yellow ventral pathway. You are caught up in a vicious cycle of isolation and suffering.

The way through this is to carefully increase social engagement even when it feels scary. Through the practices in this book, you are slowly inviting your body to awaken to more connection with others. While your ANS may say no because of faulty neuroception, you can use your head, your top-down processing, to gently work with your nervous system. When we have diverging agendas, we can invite both top-down and bottom-up processing.

As you move through the book with your partner you will begin to feel better; more able to look someone in the eye. You will know that you are moving out of the trauma feedback loop when you seek out a trusted person in times of suffering, and you feel the nourishment of their presence. You are not alone.

5. Coregulation: Bodies/Environments Are Alive and Coregulating

Being dependent on others is being human. The Western world sets us up to believe that each individual must strive to become a self-regulating being. We think we are successful when we function independently of others. "Every man for himself" is a familiar motto in our hypermasculine culture. "Survival of the fittest" underlies our capitalistic climate, even when it is becoming increasingly clear that no one is safe until we are all safe enough.

Polyvagal Theory suggests a very different understanding of what it means to be a human being. Porges's theory reveals lessons that come from the body, specifically the autonomic nervous system. From an ANS perspective, the body does not function as a separate unit, independent of its surroundings. Our bodies are deeply interconnected. As living organisms, we coregulate with each other's nervous systems and with the natural world.

We see this clearly in parent/child relationships and with romantic partners. If one person becomes dysregulated, they can be soothed and downregulated by the other person's ventral response. If the soothing is unsuccessful, both persons' physiological states can become dysregulated. In other words, our bodies read and respond to each other's cues of safety and connection.

We are designed to seek safety in closeness with other people. We feel nourished in safe relationships. Many of you on this journey did not receive enough soothing, or the soothing that you did receive was disrupted by others. This is why it is so important to find an FSPM partner and/or group. Together you coregulate each other's nervous systems, giving you the opportunity to rewire, healing one step at a time.

SUMMARY

Chapter 2 gives an overview of the FSPM graphic versions. It starts by explaining how Dr. Porges discovered the dorsal vagus, a key concept in Polyvagal Theory. This changed the way that we understand the ANS. We explore neuroception, our body's safety monitor, through presenting the graphic FSPM client 7 F states and clinician models. A detailed description of each state is provided, enabling you to become familiar with how each state feels in your body. Practice 4 helps you to become familiar with the first skill: recognizing and retuning your nervous system states. We then discuss five lessons in Polyvagal Theory, including;

1. Safety first: Safety is the bedrock. None of us are safe unless all of us are safe.
2. Interoception: Honor your mind/body connection.
3. Neuroception: Our body's wisdom is designed to seek safety.
4. Social engagement: We need each other to feel safe and connected, and to heal.
5. Coregulation: Bodies/environments are alive and coregulating.

CHAPTER 3

Polyvagal Informed Focusing and the Felt Sense (Practices 6–9)

NEUROCEPTION/INTEROCEPTION

As you are practicing Skill One, recognizing and retuning your ANS, you are slowly and gently beginning to tap into body wisdom. Pause and appreciate how incredible it is that your body knows how to shift, without thinking, into autonomic states that enable you to survive threatening experiences. This natural bodily process, called neuroception, is followed by another natural process called interoception.

Skill Two, finding the felt sense, is an interoceptive process. Interoception is our sense of awareness of bodily sensation and feelings. It is often compared to intuition. Along with vision, hearing, smell, taste, and touch, Porges (2011) suggests that we have a sixth sense, interoception. Remember the long vagus nerve that is so important in Polyvagal Theory? This is the bidirectional pathway that carries information from our bodily sensations and feelings up to our brain: our brain/body connector. Focusing/felt sensing is a process that facilitates interoception as we pause and listen to all our senses. In Focusing we go inside and ask the question: "How am I today?" That includes our thoughts, feelings, physical sensations, and memories. We invite bodily awareness of a felt sense to form.

These are the two natural body processes that form the foundation of the Felt Sense Polyvagal Model (FSPM). Once you learn these two skills you become

connected to the yellow pathway of ventral energy, free of addiction and dissociation (see Figures 2.1 and 2.2).

FINDING FOCUSING

In the 1980s, I went searching for a more embodied method of treatment because
I could see that talk therapy alone was not helping my clients. The triggers that
were haunting them were not resolved by simply talking. Their suffering was
held deeply in their bodies: in facial expressions, constriction or collapse of muscle tension, the rhythm of breath flow, and their capacity for connection with me
and others. It became clear to me over time that bodies speak in many languages
that manifest in wordless movement and shape.

Finding Focusing, the work of Eugene Gendlin, provided the key to understanding how healing happens in the body. Gendlin wrote his best-selling book
Focusing back in 1978. Since that time his work has been applied to many areas
of life. While Focusing is a natural process, it can be taught as a contemplative
practice. Once you learn it, your body will bring it into all areas of your life.
People use it in education, religious practice, physical therapies, creative arts, as a
philosophy (the philosophy of the implicit), and as a methodology for developing
theory (thinking at the edge).

Gendlin also developed a method of psychotherapy and published *Focusing
Oriented Psychotherapy* in 1996. More recently it has become popular with people
who work as coaches. It's a foundational embodied practice that enhances all
kinds of experiencing.

Focusing Partners: A Coregulating Practice

We all know people with whom it is best not to share anything that matters to
us. If we have experienced something exciting, and if we tell it to those people, it
will seem almost dull. If we have a secret, we will keep it safe from those people,
safe inside us, untold. That way it won't shrivel up and lose all the meaning it has
for us. But, if you are lucky, you know one person with whom it is the other way
around. If you tell that person something exciting, it becomes more exciting. A
great story will expand, you will find yourself telling it in more detail, finding
the richness of all the elements, more than when you only thought about it alone.

Whatever matters to you, you save it until you can tell it to that person. Focusing and listening are like that: like talking to a person who makes your experience expand. In Focusing you must be that kind of person within yourself. And you can also be that way with others and show them how to be that way for you. (Gendlin, 1978/1981, p. 131)

This quote illustrates the most important point about Focusing partnerships. Coregulating with a partner not only deepens the Focusing process, but it also helps you to learn how to deepen your own connection with yourself. Recall Lesson Five in Polyvagal Theory from Chapter 2, where we discussed how our bodies are designed to coregulate with other people's nervous systems. Our Focusing partnership heals our ANS as we move toward a more ventral state.

Focusing is unique as a form of contemplative practice because we most often do it in partnerships. As safety develops you can sit across from your partner with face-to-face contact. In this open bodied way, you enhance the activation of the social engagement system and your felt sense experience. This happens when bodies connect through partners' deep listening to each other. In day-to-day life, this can happen when you share something with your best friend, and they listen with compassion. Suddenly you feel better and lighter, even though the problem hasn't changed. You are clearer regarding what to do about it. This is how we experience Focusing in a natural way with our friends and family.

In a Focusing community we spend equal time learning how to Focus and listen. This creates a powerful energy between partners. In our international community people form lifelong Focusing partnerships. They sometimes Focus on the phone or meet up online.

Guidelines for Focusing Partnerships

1. Find a consistent and uninterrupted time and frequency for your meetings. That way you don't have to negotiate each time. It is advisable to start with at least weekly meetings.
2. Stick to the same amount of time for each person. Typically 20 to 30 minutes each. This allows for a fair process.
3. Find a private space, like the space that you use in working with this book.
4. Agree on confidentiality.

5. No advice giving—stay with the spirit of deep embodied listening.

6. If you have an issue with your partnership, seek help from an experienced Focuser.

Focusing Alone

It is important to be able to connect with the felt sense on your own as well as with a partner/therapist. You may choose to have a formal practice, much like people do with meditation. However, when you become skilled in the process it becomes a way of living. You do not have to sit down and go through the steps to connect with your body wisdom. Time in and time out are seamless when you are living in a safe enough state most of the time. You learn to pause and notice when you feel yourself getting dysregulated, perhaps dissociating or craving. In that pause, you begin to find awareness and connection with your inner embodied felt sense, the Flock part of you that consciously chooses to stay grounded and connected to your healing path.

What we are emphasizing here is that while you may Focus alone, it is almost always better to partner so that you are connecting with the social engagement system, that powerful healing system in the body. Remember, the ventral state of health and growth requires social connection, and while that is avoided with trauma/addiction, it is the medicine in healing.

GENDLIN'S SIX STEPS OF FOCUSING

Below are the six steps of Focusing as Gendlin (1978/1981) developed them, and Practice 6 will walk you through each step. Remember that he only created them to help people connect with the felt sense. You do not need to use the six steps once you become familiar with the felt sense in your body. I still refer to the steps because they remain helpful in learning more about how to tap into body wisdom. Step 1, clearing space, is where mindfulness and Focusing meet. It can be used on its own as well as part of a Focusing practice.

1. **Clearing a space**: Ask yourself, what's getting in the way of feeling fine? Let your body answer. Name the issue without going into it. Take each one and place it at the right distance.

2. **Finding a felt sense**: Pick one problem and notice what you sense in your body. Allow the whole of the situation to form, thoughts, feelings, physical sensations, memories. Notice the murkiness of it.

3. **Getting a handle**: Choose a word, phrase, image, or gesture that captures the quality of the felt sense.

4. **Resonating**: Mirror back the handle, checking it with the felt sense. Pause with the sense of matching between the handle and felt sense.

5. **Asking**: Be curious, ask questions into the felt sense. What is the worst of it? What does it need? Is it okay to stay with it?

6. **Welcoming**: Pause and expand the felt sense and felt shift. Be glad it spoke to you.

*Practice 6. Skill Two: Finding the Felt Sense: The Six Steps of Focusing

I suggest you first read through the steps with your eyes open, letting your sense of neuroception become familiar with the practice. When you feel ready, you might start by reviewing Practice 2 (Noticing the Space Around You) so you have a sense of feeling grounded in your body. Choose an issue that is not too difficult to work with in the beginning.

You can also read through the six steps, and then go on to Practice 7 (A Felt Sense of the Safe Nest) where you create a safe nest felt sense. Let your body decide where it would like to start. Remember, we are not on a linear journey. You will return to each of the practices and use them as they seem relevant at the time.

Step 1: Clearing A Space

Let your body guide you into sitting or standing in your private space. Gently soften your gaze and turn attention inwards. Say hello to whatever is there. Invite yourself to take a deep breath, following your awareness down somewhere into the center of your body. Ask yourself: "How am I today? What is coming between me and feeling okay?" Often four or five issues will be there in your life. Name the issues one by one, without going into them. Take each one at a time and imagine that you are putting it out in the hall, or even further away. You can come back to any one of these later. But for now, we want to make a clear space inside, to breathe.

If one is particularly sticky, imagine floating it up into the air or putting it in on an island. Let the issue know that you will return to it again. Just for now, we welcome a cleared space.

Eventually, with practice, your body will feel clear and calm. Notice that. You can stop here and rest in your cleared space, or proceed to Step 2.

Step 2: Finding a Felt Sense

Take time to ask your inside self which of the issues that you have cleared would like your attention now. Which feels the most in need, the most urgent or tense? Or which one do you feel ready to face? Maybe your issue comes in a tightness in your body or a powerful emotion. When one emerges ask your body what this whole problem feels like. Don't answer in words: just let your inner sense of it form. Notice how you feel. Ask yourself what thoughts come. Are there memories that start to emerge? Do you notice physical sensations? As you learn to slow down and be quiet with your inside self a felt sense will form. It is easy for the head to start chatting away. Just ignore this. You will learn what to pay attention to. Bring your attention back to the center of your body. Invite yourself to stay here with a gentle, curious attitude. The felt sense is often vague and uncomfortable, so it is not something we normally notice. Let yourself linger here.

Step 3: Getting a Handle

What is the quality of the felt sense? Is it warm, tight, scared? Is there a word, phrase, color, image, or sometimes a movement that comes in your body? What captures the essence of it? This is what we call the handle. In this third step you may notice your issue begins to take a particular shape as you stay with it. It may begin to feel different from what you thought about it before you started Focusing; different from anything that you could have figured out in your head. The handle helps you to tap into body wisdom, to know the felt sense with more clarity. The difference may be small and subtle and perhaps puzzling. It feels new and fresh. This is what we are looking for; something that comes with a bit of a body shift. This step helps you to formulate or symbolize the experience. Saying aloud the qualities of the felt sense enhances and sometimes accesses the meaning of the experience. As things begin to become clearer you understand yourself a little bit more. Often the handle doesn't make linear sense. It can sound poetic. That's because it comes from the body.

Step 4: Resonating Felt Sense and Handle: Checking With Body Wisdom

Take the handle word or phrase and check it against the felt sense. In this step we make sure, as you or your partner say it back, that it resonates well with your body. This back and forth is where you will feel your body's knowing. It knows when you have the right handle because your body knows when you don't have it right! Your partner may repeat your handle back to you and it may not fit.

"Relaxed tingling?" "No, not quite tingling." "Relaxed humming?" "Yes, that's it! Humming."

It's very important to let your partner know if you need to take time here to sit with the felt sense and let the handle form just as it needs to.

Step 5: Asking

As you stay with your bodily felt sense and the handle, you can be curious about it. What part feels relaxed, and where in your body do you feel the tingling? What about this whole problem makes you feel tingly? What does this place need? Or what would it feel like in your body without all of this?

You can ask questions that help to get the right closeness or distance from the felt sense. Here it is important to notice how your autonomic state is interacting with your felt sense. For example, if you are in Flight/Fight, you can ask if it is okay to be with all of this. Do you need to back up from it? If you are in a Freeze or Fold state you can ask if it is okay to come closer to it. If so, you can ask it what the worst of it is. Asking is a powerful step that requires skill in finding the right questions and the right time to be with what might be too scary and intense, or too far away and numb.

If you find yourself going into the head, gently ask your body to go back into the felt sense. This step is particularly powerful when a skilled listener can help you go deeper into your felt sense. As you deepen your level of experiencing you are activating the ventral vagus, allowing for somatic integration of your traumatic memories. This is the power of Focusing partnerships: the power of coregulation to enhance the healing journey.

Step 6: Receiving

Here we slow down once again, pausing to notice all that has come in this Focusing session. Take time to welcome whatever has come. The most uncomfortable places tell us the most about how we are living our lives. Enjoy the new embodied awareness. Let yourself resonate with the felt shift if one comes. Notice how your body carries it. This step can bring you to a deep level of experiencing, a true moment of awe and wonder. Sometimes it feels profound, like a spiritual or creative awakening. Pause . . . and honor your body's wisdom.

An important note here: It is very common not to experience a significant felt shift, particularly if you are working on traumatic experiences. If you take your time to notice tiny movements, knowing that each time you visit these uncomfortable places you are building new neuropathways of healing.

There are different ways to work with the Felt Sense.

In Focusing practice, we work with the felt sense in a myriad of ways. Sometimes we go inside and find a felt sense that helps us to ground in more safety. This is an important aspect of what I call *Polyvagal Informed Focusing*, because we pay particular attention to neuroception, the primacy of the need for safety. Practice 7 (A Felt Sense of the Safe Nest) is like this. We look for safety and connection, a grounded sense of self. Then we use these experiences as a resource when we feel in need of some good ventral energy.

Other times we Focus on a specific problem, like in the traditional way of following the six steps in Practice 6. And sometimes we just drop down inside to be with ourselves in a deeper way, with no agenda.

THE HEART OF FOCUSING: THE FELT SHIFT

When a handle comes it is often accompanied by a physical release, an Aha! Or a "Yes, that's it" awakening. We call this a felt shift. The shift offers a whole new way of understanding the situation. While shifts often occur with the handle, they can also occur anytime throughout the focusing process.

You feel better mainly because your body feels better, freer, released. The whole body is alive in a less constricted way. You have localized a problem that had previously made your whole body feel bad. An immediate freeing feeling lets you know there is a body shift. It is the body having moved toward a solution (Gendlin, 1978, p. 29).

Gendlin speaks of the release of a constricted place in the body that shifts into a freeing feeling (1978). The FSPM proposes that this is the body's way of shifting states in the autonomic nervous system. The shift moves us from a tight flight/fight sympathetic state to a calm safe ventral vagal state, or from a dead-end, numb, dorsal vagus state through the sympathetic and back to the ventral vagus. Listening to the felt shift in your nervous system (neuroception) and your embodied awareness (interoception), guides you in your own bodily knowing. You become the expert in knowing what you need to heal. It is the heart of focusing and body wisdom in action!

Felt shifts can be small and subtle, or enormous waves of experiencing, and as mentioned above, they don't always come during a Focusing round. The process remains alive in the body and evolves over time. A next round of Focusing may carry it forward again, building new neuropathways.

Many therapies today add a body scan as a way of incorporating a somatic dimension to their methodology. Clearly, body scans do not involve the active development of the felt sense/felt shift. They only go halfway into the body. The other half is the listening for direction through the wonders of the felt sense/shift.

THE ADDICTIVE SHIFT/THE TRAUMA FEEDBACK LOOP

Addictive shifts happen in the ANS too. Remember the trauma feedback loop. Aided by addictive behaviors the body propels from sympathetic to dorsal and back in an endless, hopeless loop of survival. The felt sense is not present in an addicted shift. While there is a physical release in the body, it does not carry your life forward. As we see on the FSPM 7 F states model (Figure 2.1), the addicted cycle is in the upper half, the emotionally dysregulated part of the cycle. When you practice Skill One, recognizing and rewiring your ANS state, you can visually see and map out your current state, the place where you need to be, and what you need to do to get there.

In the beginning of finding the felt sense, it can be very confusing for your body to learn the difference between addictive shifts and felt sense shifts. They both bring relief, that's why you become addicted. But the dead end of addiction carries life processes around and around in an endless, vicious cycle. The felt sense, on the other hand, carries the magic of body wisdom.

Practice 7. A Felt Sense of the Safe Nest

(Some people don't like the word *safe*, so find a word that works for you: *grounded, okay, competent* . . .)

Let's begin by finding a private space. Settle yourself in your chair, or you might want to stand up. Soften your gaze, and if it feels right, you can close your eyes. Remember that you can come back to the room at any time and find your comforting object.

See if you can find a moment in your life when you felt calm, content, or grounded. Maybe you are connected with a person, a pet, the land around you. It doesn't have to be perfect, just a time that felt okay. Maybe it's when you feel competent at work. If it is hard to find, I invite you to imagine one. Where are you? Are you alone, or who is with you? What is the story? If it feels okay, notice where this place lives in your body: your chest, throat, belly. Your body may begin to shift into a calmer, more grounded state. This is the beginning of your felt sense, of a safe nest in which to do this work.

Notice if there is a word, phrase, image, or gesture that captures the quality of your experience. This is your handle, or bookmark, for the felt sense. Remembering your handle helps you to use this felt sense when you need to find your safe nest. It could be the words "smoky blue," or the smell of your grandmothers' perfume, "sweet aliveness," or a large tree in your backyard, "gnarly home." Your body may move and sway as you find this place. Don't worry if your handle sounds funny or doesn't make sense, like "swirling calm." The body has its own language, often paradoxical. Bodies know how to hold complexity. As we begin to round this off inside, pause and honor whatever comes.

Welcome to your embodied knowing! Practices 6 and 7 have helped you to start your Focusing journey. These practices will deepen and become a resource that you come back to as we move through the book.

It's important to take time to write in your journal a Process Recording of your felt sense experience. In your Process Recording you can describe your thoughts, feelings, physical sensations, and memories as they relate to your focusing experience. You may want to describe your handle, if you had a shift, and any action steps that came to you. Some people write a poem or draw an image of their experience. The recording is your unique way of tracking your focusing journey.

GENDLIN'S EXPERIENCING SCALE

The Experiencing Scale (Gendlin et al., 1969) was created by Eugene Gendlin as a result of his psychotherapy research. You can find reference to it in the Clinician Model of the FSPM (Figure 2.2). The scale appears down the left-hand side of the model from number one through seven. It is a powerful assessment tool that measures seven states of experiencing. Reliability and validity were developed for the scale, and judges were trained through standardized materials. Each level represents a deeper connection to felt sensing. For clients, the easiest way to understand it is to use the graded yellow coloring of the model as a guide for assessing how deeply you are connecting to your bodily felt sense. The deeper the yellow, the deeper your felt sense of presence and coregulation. For practitioners, the scale is a helpful way to track your clients interoceptive awareness by rating their level of experiencing over time.

There are several examples of the Experiencing Scale. Here is the one that we use:

1. The client simply talks about events, ideas, or other people.
2. The client refers to self but without expressing emotions.
3. The client expresses emotions but only as they relate to
   external circumstances.
4. The client focuses directly on emotions and thoughts about the self.
5. The client engages in an exploration of their inner experience (felt sense).
6. The client gains awareness of previously implicit feelings and meanings
   (felt shift).
7. The client has an ongoing process of in-depth self-understanding, which
   provides new perspectives to solve significant problems (felt sense).

Ventral States: Levels 1 through 7 (Flowing, Flock, Fun, Fired Up)

If your client is presenting in a ventral state you can expect to see a range of levels, from 1 through 7, depending on how deeply they are connecting with experiencing. For example, often at the beginning of a session when a client is retelling a story, they want to tell you the details of a situation and don't slow down to deeply connect. As the session progresses, we invite a deeper level of experiencing to develop and we see the client progress into Levels 5, 6, and 7 as they connect with the felt sense/shift. The ventral state is reflected in a full range of experiencing.

Dorsal States: Levels 1 and 2 (Fold)

The dorsal shutdown state is disconnected from sympathetic and ventral energy. This dissociated state constricts affect, resulting in the very limited range of Levels 1 and 2.

Sympathetic States: Levels 3 and 4 (Fight/Flight)

Your client can move into connecting with feeling, but spins around in flight/ fight, unable to pause and feel into a felt sense of the whole situation. This results in a chaotic, flooding state of hypervigilance. Felt sense is not available in this state, the range of experiencing is constricted, reflected in the absence of Levels 5, 6, or 7.

As a client you may or may not be interested in using the Experiencing Scale in your Focusing sessions. Some folks find this kind of information helpful, and others don't.

IAN'S SAFE NEST, A POLYVAGAL INFORMED (PI) FOCUSING ORIENTED THERAPY SESSION

Below is an example of a Polyvagal Informed Focusing oriented therapy session where we are using the FSPM and the Experiencing Scale. Notice how we start with neuroception and then move into the interoceptive Focusing steps. This example helps you to see the process in action.

I open the door to my waiting area and see Ian. He doesn't look up, so he doesn't see me. I feel a gentle pulling in the center of my body. Like when you see a person you care about, who looks vulnerable, deeply troubled. Ian's body slumps down beside the palm tree in the corner. He folds into himself.

This is our fourth session. So far, we are just beginning the journey of creating enough safety for Ian to let me into his struggle. He keeps coming back, and for that I am grateful. His journey is pretty nasty. In a detached way he has shared some facts about his story. A physically abusive father. A mom who shut down and drank a lot to manage her fear of her husband. Two older brothers who coped in opposite ways. The oldest raged (fight). The middle brother panicked (flight). Ian numbed (fold).

We enter my office and settle into our familiar seats. He often slumps down into the couch, but today Ian surprises me. He sits up, looks right at me, and says "Hi." Wow, I am delighted. I ask him how his week was. "Okay," he says. While it's hard to imagine, Ian plays sax in a jazz band. When he told me this in the first session, I looked him up online and watched him playing. I could see the deeply embodied way that he caressed his instrument. Here was the doorway into Ian's felt sense.

I invite him to revisit Skill One and check to see where he is in the 7 F's. He closes his eyes. He is becoming pretty good at connecting with the slow, dorsal energy in his body. I introduce the safe nest practice and invite Ian gently down inside. My hunch is right. When I ask him to find an experience where he feels safe and grounded his body leads him to a recent experience where he is playing his saxophone. Ian's whole body changes as he shifts into a more ventral state. He appears looser and stronger at the same time. His handle for the safe nest is "swerving," with a body gesture of swaying back and forth. Together we stand up and began to move. As I resonate the handle Ian says, "Swaying and swerving." Together we coregulate in the relational felt sense of safety. So amazing!

A week later Ian shows up folded inward again. But this time my body remembers his handle, swaying and swerving. I remind him of the words as we settle in, and a gorgeous little smile forms at the corners of his mouth. I love these moments of deep connection. He says, "I recognize I've slipped back into the familiar dorsal state over the week. But you are reminding me of ventral." He is learning how to rewire. Now we are ready to visit the difficult places, with the help of the six steps of Focusing.

IAN'S SIX STEPS, SKILL TWO

1. Clearing a Space

I ask Ian the question: "Is there anything coming between you and feeling okay right now?" He closes his eyes and brings attention down inside. He notices something big, and he practices putting it in a balloon and floating it up to the clouds. We continue with four other issues that are bothering him, and he manages to clear them with balloons or boxes. He rests in the cleared space.

2. Finding a Felt Sense: Experience Scale 3 to 4

Ian's body chooses one issue to bring back inside, and he takes his time to be with all of it. The issue is about his fear of his brother. As he stays with it, a large gray cloud lands heavily on his chest and spreads downwards to his ankles. It won't budge. I ask him if the cloud is familiar. "Yes, I know this feeling in my body. I almost always feel it when I am with my older brother, and other times too. It is a feeling of Fixate/Freeze."

We stay with it for a while. He says, "I have always been afraid of him. I feel like he runs my life, he is the gray cloud. He is the master of me."

3. Getting a Handle: Experience Scale 4 to 5

I ask Ian if he can find a word, image, or gesture that captures this place. "Braced silence," he says. I notice his face tightening and suddenly his chest heaves as he begins to cry. Big sighs as we welcome the tears. As the felt sense opens more a felt shift begins to occur. He moves from Fixate/Freeze into the beginning of a ventral pathway. His body is releasing the tension in the gray cloud.

4. Resonating

I say back, "You know this place. Fear of your brother. Braced silence." Ian nods in agreement. More tears come as I resonate. Heaving, opening his whole chest area, releasing constriction. I see his body relax into the couch. He opens his arms more, facial muscles relax. Resting his head on the couch, breathing deeply, he stays inside attending to what is there.

5. Asking

After a while I gently drop the question down inside: "What does this place need?"

"I see myself when I am 6 and my brother is yelling at me. That little guy needs rescuing. I need to protect him from my brother. Even now, I need to keep my distance from him." Ian stays there, pausing inside. "I am holding him; he is so small." Another pause. Ian's body appears more relaxed. He smiles, "I am remembering swaying and swerving. I feel strong when I play my saxophone. That part of me can help the little boy."

6. Welcoming: Experience Scale 6 to 7

"Yes," I say. "That part of you has so much to offer the little boy. What is happening in your body now?" Ian stays inside, quiet, for several minutes of silence. I see his breathing expand and settle, his face is relaxed, glowing—a truly Flowing state.

"I feel calm and more alive. Wow!" Ian slowly opens his eyes and notices what is around him as he comes back from a deeply embodied healing journey. He went to places that likely wouldn't have emerged so early on in therapy without the help of body wisdom.

"You know, I am also becoming more aware of how I go to Fawning with my brother. It's like, I am waking up and realizing that I do whatever it takes to get away from him."

We take that new knowing down inside. Ian asks his body if it is ready for another round of Focusing. He looks up at me and smiles, "Next time, Jan. I am exhausted. I feel good ventral energy and I want to bask in it. Let's stop here for now." We relax together basking in a moment of deep coregulation, welcoming Ian's lost boy.

We are covering a lot of terrain in this chapter—deep embodied terrain. Take your time with each practice. Pause and check to see how your body is responding. Make sure you give yourself time between each practice to let in the changes that you are experiencing.

*Practice 8. Felt Sense Polyvagal Grounding Practice

This is the foundational practice for the FSPM, bringing together the two embodied processes of interoception (felt sense) and neuroception (rewiring ANS).

Felt Sense/Polyvagal Grounding Practice (FSPGP)

I invite you to settle yourself into your chair, put down anything on your lap, or you may want to stand up. Soften your gaze or find something in the room to bring to your attention. If it feels right for you, close your eyes. Feel your feet on the floor, and slowly bring your attention into the center of your body. Say a friendly hello to your inside self.

Being with your body from the inside, notice how you are holding yourself. How is your body carrying you? Notice your muscles, your breath, your limbs. Are you held tight, anxious, and wound up in fight/flight . . . or loose and comfortable in a relaxed, grounded place . . . or heavy and lethargic, maybe depressed, or kind of numb and frozen, in dorsal?

Or maybe you are in a blending of states. Grounded in ventral, with a bit of sympathetic, a Fun or Fired Up state. Or maybe grounded in ventral with a bit of dorsal, a nice Flowing state. Or maybe shifting back and forth in Fixate/Freeze.

Invite your body to find an experience, a moment in time, that feels calm or grounded. It doesn't have to be perfect, just imagine a moment in your life when you felt okay. Things are moving along, and you have a sense of managing. You might feel a moment of connection with a person, an animal, or the natural world—a tree, a lake, the land. If a time is hard to find, I invite you to imagine one.

Are you alone, or who is with you? What is the story? Notice where this place lives in your body. Your heart, breath, shoulders, throat, jaw. Notice the smells and sounds around you. How are you feeling about what is happening? What are you thinking? Allow a felt sense to form.

Your body may begin to shift into a felt sense of grounded. Is there a word, phrase, image, or body gesture that captures the quality of your experience? In Focusing we call this the handle. It could be floaty, blue, or a sunny splash, or it can be a body gesture such as outstretched arms. Welcome whatever comes from deep inside the body, the implicit world. As we begin to round this off, you can slowly bring yourself back to the room, opening your eyes, feeling your feet on the floor and your sitting bones in the chair. Make a Process Recording. In Practice 9 you will complete a Body Card for Practice 8, your Felt Sense Polyvagal Grounding Practice.

THE FELT SENSE POLYVAGAL MODEL BODY CARDS

The FSPM Body Cards were developed over many years with input from our Focusing community. The Body Cards document the interoceptive and neuroceptive journey. There are several different options in body shape and color for you to choose from on my website at janwinhall.com. You can also add your level of experiencing.

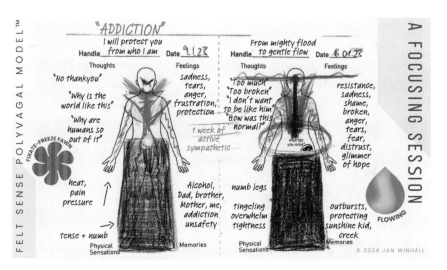

Figure 3.1: Addiction Body Card Example
Source: "Ragna Munyer, Felt Sense Polyvagal Model Facilitator"

At the top of the card, write the handle to help you remember the essence of the journey. Dating it helps to document your path over time, the places where you get stuck in your ANS pathways, and the times when you experience felt shifts in neuroception and interoception. As you accumulate Body Cards, you can lay them out in front of you and see images of your FSPM journey.

In each corner of the card, describe different avenues into the felt sense: your thoughts, feelings, physical sensations, and memories. You can use color to draw the felt sense and felt shift, documenting the neuroceptive state and the felt shift, if one occurs.

Figure 3.1 shows an example of two body cards from two separate polyvagal Focusing sessions.

In the first week you see how the person describes the Fixate/Freeze state, with the black dorsal state of numb and the red/yellow sympathetic squiggly lines of tension throughout her body. This image reflects her body's ANS state as she works with a childhood memory of her addicted family. This is the path of the trauma feedback loop. It provides no ventral energy of relief. No felt shift occurs in this Focusing session. What is important here is that her body felt safe enough through coregulation with her partner; that she was able to be with this Fixate state in her body with a bit of distance and curiosity. Creating a Body Card continues the process of getting some distance from the intensity, helping her to begin the process of regulating her ANS while being with the uncomfortable feelings.

The client documents one week of active sympathetic energy between the sessions. Her next Focusing session begins in Fixate. Her Focusing partner asks the question (written in the middle of her body): "What do you need?" With that question her body experiences a felt shift from Fixate to Flow at the bottom righthand corner of the Body Card. "Sunshine kid, creek" came to her from the felt sense of safety that she associates with the creek beside her childhood home that she would go to for comfort. She did not think about the creek—her felt sense took her to this ventral pathway of healing from a traumatic childhood. She repeats Focusing rounds in her daily practice paying attention to this wounded place.

Here is the client's Process Recording of this session:

Going in I encounter a lot of energy in my stomach area. Tears welling up, I feel resistance to meet it. I orientate, clear space, then going back in I am flooded with sympathetic energy in my stomach, chest, then my whole upper body. My legs again are detached from the active experience. Fold, no sense of tension or any experience.

I feel resistance to my sympathetic, fighting the fight energy. I don't want to be like him. Tears stream with that sentence. Memories of outbursts at home, rages, me saving my 2-year-old sister, my cat, my brother from him, I keep them all in a good mood as much as I can. I am deeply shaken with sadness and notice my hands comforting at the ear, cheeks, it feels young. How did I believe this was normal?

Shame comes up for the tears and the crying being a lot. Too much. I don't want to be seen broken. I feel sad, shameful. A lot of active energy that I can't put into a state of nervous system. Looking back, it's probably fixate/freeze, no shift.

My arms tingle, I feel little. My face makes a contempt movement on the corner of my mouth. My finger touches it softly, wants it to soften. I remember my comforting technique in stressful situations, the biting of my inner cheeks, pushing my fingers against them.

I feel calm. Flow and Fold pendulating—I must open my eyes; I feel very vulnerable. I breathe and move, orientate, flow takes space with stillness and joy. Reflecting with my Focusing partner, I move into a grateful ventral state. So tender, so open, so revealing. I am grateful to my body for carrying all of this until I am ready to hold it myself. (Anonymous)

Using the Body Cards as a visual cue helps her body remember the interoceptive and neuroceptive journey toward healing. In this way, Body Cards enhance the neural exercise of ventral regulation. In preparation for Practice 9, Making Your FSPM Body Cards, have some colored pencils or crayons ready with a copy of the downloaded Body Cards from my website: janwinhall.com.

*Practice 9. Making Your FSPM Body Cards

Come into your quiet private space and prepare to do Practice 8, the Felt Sense Polyvagal Grounding Practice (see above). After you finish, make a Body Card. This will be a resource for you when you are searching for ventral energy.

SUMMARY

This chapter introduces you to the world of interoception, and Skill Two in the model, finding the felt sense. An introduction to Eugene Gendlin, the father of

Focusing, is followed by a description of Focusing partnerships. The six steps of Focusing are described, with a Focusing practice that helps you to create a safe nest in which to do this work.

A description of Gendlin's Experiencing Scale helps you assess how in touch you are with your felt sense. The case example of Ian illustrates the application of the Felt Sense Polyvagal Model. He learns to use the 7 F's and the 6 Steps of Focusing to activate an interoceptive state of deep embodied processing as he works through a trauma memory.

The Felt Sense Polyvagal Grounding Practice is presented as a foundational practice for the FSPM with the introduction of the Body Cards. A case example of how to use the Body Cards and Process Recording is provided.

CHAPTER 4

The Very Bad Habit of Addiction (Practices 10–12)

Some of you reading this chapter may not see yourself as a person who struggles with addiction. You may be reading this book because you know that you are struggling with a traumatic history that has resulted in your numbing, zoning out, and perhaps falling into destructive relationships. Addictions result in and are fueled by numbing, so much of what you read about in this chapter will be relatable to you as you explore your history of dissociation and living in the trauma feedback loop. As you go through the practices, I encourage you to notice how they may relate to your own experience. **There is much to learn for all of us about how trauma and addiction correlate.**

DEFINING ADDICTION: SICK OR BAD?

There are many ways that cultures have understood addiction: It's a moral failing, reflective of bad people making bad choices, it's a quest for self-medication to relieve suffering, it's a result of childhood attachment trauma, it's a choice. Some Indigenous cultures see addictions as medicines that help you when the pain is unbearable.

Our top-down Western culture shifted its understanding from a moral failing model to a sickness model in the 1990s during the decade of the brain.

The advent of fMRI's new research revealed changes in brain chemistry of those struggling with addiction. As a result, the medical community advocated for a new understanding of addiction as a chronic brain disease.

While both models fail to reflect the wisdom of the body, they are powerful explanations in that they shine a light on different aspects of the state of addiction. For example, while brain disease can be the consequence of addiction, it doesn't explain the root cause. And while people who are addicted can do bad things, they are not bad people.

Let's pause here. This is a painful place for many of you. Facing the harm that you have caused yourself and those around you is a very tough part of healing. While it is vitally important to take responsibility for your behavior, it can feel overwhelming. When you shift to an embodied understanding it makes it much easier to make sense of your actions, and to develop deep compassion for yourself.

Remember two things. First, **addictions occur in survival mode**, when you are disconnected from the ventral Flock pathway of social engagement. In survival mode humans lose contact with the part of us that cares about others. Second, **we are more than our behavior**. Our behavior does not define all of who we are. We are capable of drastically changing our behaviors, but we remain the same person. These two things are not excuses; they are explanations to remind yourself when you feel the shame of your actions. You can draw comfort from knowing that the more you engage in the Felt Sense Polyvagal Model (FSPM) practices, the more socially connected you become, and the more you can live a life of integrity.

We will delve into this more in the next chapter on trauma when we work with the critic. For now, take a deep breath, and try to be compassionate with yourself. Practice saying to yourself, *"Addictions occur in survival mode, and I am more than my behavior."* You can go to Practice 8 (The Felt Sense Polyvagal Grounding Practice) if you need to.

While the disease model has become the language of mental health professionals, the shame many of you carry in your body is evidence of the fact that the moral failing model is still alive and well. It is also clear in the way that we treat those who are caught using drugs and alcohol. Our ambivalence shows up in the mixture of legal and medical treatment responses. It appears our culture just can't decide whether addicted folks are sick or bad.

The main message in the Felt Sense Polyvagal Model is that you are neither sick nor bad: your body is responding instinctively to threat. You are simply doing what your brain/body has learned to do to survive at all costs.

A NEW DEFINITION: ADDICTION IS A LEARNED HABIT

The FSPM proposes a new definition of addiction that embraces somatic awareness.

In developing the model, I went searching for a new way of understanding that reflected the adaptive features of trauma/addiction responses. The model needed an explanation that shifted the paradigm away from sickness and blame, thus honoring the protective features of body wisdom. Marc Lewis's wonderful book, *The Biology of Desire: Why Addiction is Not a Brain Disease* (2015), provides a nonpathologizing learning model of addiction. The learning model of addiction updates our pathologizing paradigm because it reflects cutting edge neuroscience research into neuroplasticity and feedback loops.

NEUROPLASTICITY: BRAINS ARE ALWAYS CHANGING

Put simply, neuroplasticity is the idea that brains are continuously changing. This is significant because prior to the decade of the brain it was thought that brain anatomy was fixed and hardwired; our brain only changed with aging, disease, or injury. Scientists thought that when brain cells were lost, they could not be replaced. Treatment for brain injury was very limited. But with the advent of sophisticated neuroimaging machines, this idea was disproven. It became clear that cells were reproducing all the time. The brain is constantly growing and changing!

This knowledge led neuroplasticity researchers to design a series of new treatment strategies. Their investigations revealed stunning results. Engaging the brain in neural exercises led to the development of new neuropathways. Patients regained skills they had lost due to strokes or other brain injury. This proved that the brain could continue to grow, change, and heal in ways that were previously thought impossible. This knowledge was revolutionary and has changed the way we think about treating illness, injury, and addiction. The learning model acknowledges the brain's capacity to heal itself, thus providing a hopeful future for addiction treatment.

As with all revolutionary thinking, it was met with skepticism. Merzenich (Doidge, 2017), one of the main neuroplasticity researchers, noted that the mainstream of neuroscience thought this was sort of *semi-serious* stuff. His colleagues criticized the quality of the experiments, saying that they were sloppy. Merzenich examined them in depth and concluded that the position of his colleagues was arrogant and indefensible (Doidge, 2017).

This is important because it points to the fear and consequent reluctance of many to embrace a paradigm shift. As we embark on the Felt Sense Polyvagal Model of Trauma and Addiction we are at the forefront of a new revolution in honoring and reclaiming the wisdom of the body. Being a part of this movement, together, is healing. While it takes courage to speak about it, we see how new ideas like neuroplasticity become accepted with time and patience. If you are intrigued to delve into this area more, Norman Doidge's book *The Brain That Changes Itself* is a wonderful journey into the neuroplastic revolution (Doidge, 2007).

ADDICTION AND NEUROPLASTICITY: AN "INEVITABLE FEATURE OF THE BASIC HUMAN DESIGN"

Marc Lewis argues that addiction is not a disease, but rather the result of neuroplasticity. He states:

> Addiction results, rather, from the motivated repetition of the same thoughts and behaviors until they become habitual. Thus, addiction develops—it's learned—but it's learned more deeply and often more quickly than most other habits, due to a narrowing tunnel of attention and attraction. A close look at the brain highlights the role of desire in this process. The neural circuitry of desire governs anticipation, focused attention, and behavior. So, the most attractive goals will be pursued repeatedly, while other goals lose their appeal, and that *repetition* (rather than the drugs, booze, or gambling) will change the brains' wiring. As with other developing habits, this process is grounded in a neurochemical feedback loop that's present in all normal brains. But it cycles more persistently because of frequent recurrence of desire and the shrinking range of what is desired. Addiction arises from the same feelings that bind lovers to each other and children to their parents. And it builds

on the same cognitive mechanisms that get us to value short-term gains over long-term benefits. Addiction is unquestionably destructive, yet it is uncannily normal, an inevitable feature of the basic human design. (2015, p. xii)

The sickness model argues that addiction is a brain disease because it changes brain chemistry. Lewis points out that this change process, called neuroplasticity, is present in cell density, shape and size of the cortex, gene expression, and with all activities involving learning and development. Neuroplasticity is present in all new skill development, like learning how to add and subtract, how to read and learn from this book, how to heal from brain injury, trauma, and addiction. Therefore, the kind of brain change we see in an addicted brain would have to be pathological for us to think of it as a disease. Right?

But this is a key point in the learning model; the kind of brain change seen in addiction is no different than the process that occurs when we become passionate about something or someone. When we become absorbed in a sport, or a religion, or a political party, our brain is following the same neuropathways that are present in addiction. This is also true when we have deep feelings of connection and love for our children or romantic partner.

This makes sense. Remember your experiences of falling in love. You think about the person all the time, hoping they will call you, daydreaming about the last time you saw them. You feel a surge of excitement when your phone rings. Much like the person struggling with addiction, you feel a sense of anticipation and reward. This is all a normal part of being in love. Similarly with our children, they are never far from our thoughts. We feel deeply connected through enduring intergenerational bonds.

FEEDBACK LOOPS: WHAT FIRES TOGETHER, WIRES TOGETHER

So how do our brains develop habits? Lewis uses the analogy of rainwater. At first rain falls randomly onto your new garden. But as time goes by you begin to see little paths or rivulets form. Eventually new rain follows the formation, taking on the shape and size of existing paths as alternative pathways diminish.

Brain patterns develop in a similar way. Brains grow randomly in the beginning, but as time goes by, they self-organize and begin to follow newly formed pathways, leading in new directions. Eventually growth slows down as patterns are formed. Those patterns become habits. Habits form feedback loops: a process in which the output of a system circles back and is used as input. This is part of normal brain development.

Some habits turn into addictions. For example, desire/wanting (the prime motivator in addiction) is self-reinforcing. The more something is reinforced with a gush of pleasure, the more we seek it out. The more we seek it out, the more a habit is formed. If too much repetition occurs, your habit becomes an addiction. The Canadian neuropsychologist Hebb (1949) coined the famous phrase: *neurons that fire together, wire together.*

Repetition is the key here. If you are eating chocolate cake at your favorite restaurant once a week when you visit your friend you may be developing a habit, something that you and your friend do together. No problem. If you start eating chocolate cake two or three times a week without your friend, you are increasing the repetitions of the habit. If it increases to a daily activity, you are on a track to becoming addicted. You can ask yourself the questions: Is it helping you in the short term, hurting you in the long term, and can you stop doing it?

THE PLASTIC PARADOX: TOO MUCH OF A GOOD THING

The plastic paradox is that the same neuroplastic properties that allow us to change our brains and produce more flexible behaviors can also allow us to produce more rigid ones.

—DOIDGE, 2017

At a crucial point neuropathways become rigid, reducing the ability to change. This happens when we repeat the same habits over and over, seeking the reward again and again. The repetition forms a neurofeedback loop that becomes too entrenched, and we fall into a rut that we cannot get out of easily. New growth is blocked by too much of a good thing. This occurs in the state of addiction.

Practicing moderation has become part of the language in addiction treatment for good reason. While increased repetition leads to the plastic paradox, or the rut, moderation prevents it.

Gendlin described addiction as a stopped process. Indeed, that is a good way of thinking about the plastic paradox. It's a stuck place both neurophysiologically and psychologically. No felt sense here.

THE TRAUMA FEEDBACK LOOP: YOUR ANS BACK-UP PLAN

Feedback loops are present in pleasurable, painful, or frightening experiences. Neural patterns based on desire can merge with those based on depression or anxiety. Gabor Maté illustrates this pathway in his seminal book *In the Realm of Hungry Ghosts: Close Encounters with Addiction* (2010), where he describes how addictive pathways are formed by traumatic experiences that motivate us to seek relief through addiction.

Referring to the graphic model of the FSPM 7 F states (Figures 2.1 and 2.2), as you look at the top half of the model you see the trauma feedback loop. This is the endless loop that forms as people shift back and forth from Flight/Fight, to Fixate/Freeze/Fawn, to Fold, and back again. The more you think scary, painful, and angry thoughts, the more neurons are firing and wiring together, the more a trauma feedback loop is forming. The lonelier you feel the more you seek out numbing behaviors to block the pain, and the more those behaviors reinforce the TFL.

While the loop is a vicious circle, it is also keeping you alive. I think of the trauma feedback loop as your ANS back-up plan. It kicks in when you feel completely overwhelmed, caught, and without escape. Like a generator that provides electricity when the lights go out, the trauma feedback loop is your body's system of survival.

The TFL is fueled by addictions. They propel you back and forth to sustain life. Your body cannot survive in sympathetic or dorsal states forever, so the propelling action of addictive behaviors is literally keeping you alive. That is something to be grateful for. That is body wisdom.

DISSOCIATION AND/OR ADDICTION?

While you may recognize that you are living in the trauma feedback loop much of the time, you may not experience yourself struggling with addictive behaviors. Some folks are aware of dissociating but haven't identified any specific behaviors that are repetitive in an addictive way. That may be the case because you just haven't been aware of them. Let me give you an example.

Sue was 20 years old when I began to see her for trauma therapy. While she did not identify as having any addictive behaviors, she described horrific experiences of abuse that caused her to numb feelings and lose time in her day-today life. As therapy progressed, she shared memories of her father yelling and throwing dishes at dinnertime. She would tremble with terror as she recalled traumatic memories. In a Focusing session her body took her back to an experience where, as a little girl, she was gazing down at the kitchen floor, counting the patterns in the red and black tiles over and over again. She realized that this behavior was helping her in some way, but she didn't know how. One day after that session she became aware that even now she would often sit on her couch in the living room and count the colored patterns on the carpet. This felt soothing at first, but often resulted in her falling asleep and missing school or watching endless hours of television.

I explained to Sue that counting patterns was a repetitious behavior that could facilitate a dissociated state. The dinner table was a very unsafe and inescapable place. As her body surged into flight/fight she unconsciously shifted into a dorsal shutdown state, aided by her counting behavior. Over time a habitual feedback loop was created by the repetitious nature of counting. Counting helped her in the short term, hurt her in the long term, and she couldn't stop doing it.

The good news is that because Sue became aware of the counting, and how it induced a dorsal deadened state, she was able with time and FSPM practices to stop the counting behavior, and to become more present in a ventral socially engaged way.

Sue would never have thought of counting as an addictive behavior, partly because she wasn't aware of it, and because for too long society has restricted the definition of addictions to be drug and alcohol related. But anyone who listens to the body knows that addictions come in all forms and sizes. Behavioral addictions follow the same neuropathways as substance addictions (Lewis, 2015). Gazing at a fish tank, repeated rubbing of parts of your body, meditation, and prayer all are ways of inducing dissociated states if they are repeated enough to create the plastic paradox; a rut too big to easily escape.

> *Take some time here to consider how your body shifts autonomic states. You may not be labeling your soothing behaviors as addictive because you have never associated them with the word addiction. This is where it is important to share with your therapist/FSPM Focusing partner to explore the nature of your habits. You can ask yourself what behaviors you engage in to numb or to stimulate a heightened state.*

IN LOVE, OR ADDICTED?

Let's go back to the example of being in love. What is the difference between a healthy relationship, fueled by a ventral feedback loop (the bottom half of the FSPM), and an addictive relationship, fueled by the TRL (top half of the FSPM)?

When you are in a socially engaged ventral loving state you feel safe in your body. You are present and alive with warm, loving feelings toward your partner. Key to assessing this state is the sense that you trust your partner to be consistent, not perfect but good enough, in their capacity to respond to your needs.

Addictive relationships feel disturbing and unsafe. What may at first have felt new and exciting, now feels scary or too unpredictable. You find yourself obsessed with someone, unable to let go in spite of the harmful aspects of the experience. You are falling into habitual patterns that violate your own sense of integrity. Abusive relationships are like this. Affairs can also be like this. You find yourself lying to your partner, as you secretly plan time with this exciting person in your life.

Remember Lewis's learning model of addiction. Your brain is being fueled by desire, a narrowing of attention that begins to form into a learned habit. This habit is part of a neurochemical feedback loop. What doesn't feed the desire to be with the partner is let go, a process called pruning. Similar to pruning dead growth off a tree, the brain lets go of unused pathways, reinforcing the feedback loop. You become more and more obsessed with the person, caught in a rut, the plastic paradox. If you are not able to detach, to stop the cycle, it becomes addictive. This is what is now called *relationship addiction*, or *love addiction*. Recall our definition of addiction: It helps you in the short term, hurts you in the long term, and you can't stop doing it.

Let's take time here to pause.

This is a lot of information to take in, especially when it may bring up all kinds of intense feelings. Remember to pace and share the process of learning with your FSPM partner/therapist. While you are learning about how trauma and addiction form in the body, you are on a healing journey with each new somatic practice.

The next practice begins the journey of exploring the roots of your experience of being soothed. This is important because when you were young and seeking out soothing behaviors, neuropathways were being formed in your brain. Those neuropathways shape subsequent behaviors and are often the beginnings of the development of addictive behaviors. What fires together wires together and forms somatic memories held in your body. We are destined to repeat those behaviors neurophysiologically and behaviorally through trauma feedback loops. In other words, they are learned habits that manifest later in life, often as triggers or behavioral addictions. We are going to dig deeper in Practice 10 (First Memories of Feeling Soothed).

*Practice 10. First Memories of Feeling Soothed

Settle yourself in your quiet, private place. Notice your breathing and say a friendly hello to your inside self. We are going to start this practice by resourcing a grounded place inside. Bring attention down into the center of your body, feeling your weight settle into the ground below you. Notice how the Earth holds you up. You are not alone.

Invite your body to find a place where you feel a sense of safety, grounding, and confidence. Maybe you have a handle for this place and a Body Card that you can visualize. Place a hand gently on the part of your body where you feel this felt sense of grounding. Take your time here to breathe, welcoming the good energy. As we go deeper you can bring this felt sense with you.

We are going back to your child self. Let your body find this part of you. Invite a time when you felt wounded, hurt, or disappointed by someone and in need of comfort. Not the worst time.

Where are you . . . ? Who is there . . . ? What is the story . . . ?

Where do you go for comfort? Is it a person, a place, a pet? Does it help you? Does it hurt you? Notice where you feel this in your body.

Where do you go now for soothing, comfort, relief? Is it similar, or different?

Invite your felt sense of grounding to be with the wounded place. Notice how your body feels into this. Your legs, arms, throat. Are you able to connect with some ventral energy? Notice if a felt shift forms. Do you have a handle for this place?

As you slowly bring yourself back to your room, you can round off your practice by welcoming whatever came.

Take some time here to write a Process Recording and/or Body Card. When you feel ready, share with your listening partner.

THE ADDICTED BRAIN: HOW GOOD PEOPLE CAN DO BAD THINGS

It can be helpful to explore how different parts of the brain are involved in addiction. It helps to further your understanding of how you fell into this rut, and how you can get out of it. And most importantly, it explains in neuroscience terms how good people can do bad things.

We will go through five main areas that Lewis (2015) describes in his learning model. A caution: Lewis points out that the brain is very complex but for the sake of simplicity he has chosen five areas.

Dorsolateral Prefrontal Cortex (DPC): "The Bridge of the Ship"

The dorsolateral prefrontal cortex (DPC) is the part of the brain that I think of as the adult, responsible self. You will find it by placing your fingers in the middle of your forehead between your eyes. Lewis calls this the bridge of the ship (2015, p. 45). It is this part of your brain that is responsible for planning, reasoning, self-regulating, and forming new habits based on a coherent sense of who you are. This part of your brain is connected to the ventral branch of the vagus nerve, promoting health, safety, and insight, all essential for healing from trauma and addiction. In other words, *this is the part of your brain that you need to be steering your life.*

Unfortunately, in the state of addiction the DPC loses its connection with the striatum, the action brain. Tragically we see the addicted person behaving in ways that are not reasonable or empathetic toward others. This part of the brain is compromised and results in people losing connection with their own integrity. The responsible, socially engaged part of the self is nowhere to be found. The addicted person is then judged as morally "bad."

Ventral Striatum (VS): Motivational Engine

The ventral striatum (VS) is what Lewis (2015) describes as the main character involved with addiction. It focuses on feelings of desire, craving, and reward. The striatum focuses on a goal, sending a signal to other parts of the brain to execute the goal through moving the body. The action brain, or striatum, learns from experience by assessing how well the goal was achieved in the past. Its job is to adjust itself to better achieve the goal in the future. So, it follows that *goals associated with the addiction become more important than goals that help you finish work tasks, pay bills, or stay faithful to your spouse.* This area of the brain is fueled by dopamine, the powerful neurotransmitter pumped up from the midbrain. Dopamine increases the firing rates of neurons, causing cravings to surge to the point where nothing else matters in your life. Important to note, dopamine is more than liking, it is about *wanting.* Dopamine determines what is most relevant and motivates the system to acquire it *at any cost*. This explains something very important. Often those struggling with addiction say that they don't even like what they are addicted to. But they are acutely aware of wanting it.

Midbrain: Dopamine Pump

The midbrain regulates dopamine production, pumping it to the striatum, prefrontal cortex, and the amygdala. It is the center of visual and auditory reflexes, coordinating movement.

Amygdala: "Emotional Spray-Paint"

The amygdala is subcortical, meaning it is a more primitive part of the brain. It pays attention to emotional cues, responding immediately to fear, excitement, and pleasure. Lewis refers to this part of the brain as "emotional spray-paint" (2015, p. 79). It controls the fight/flight/freeze response of the sympathetic branch of the autonomic nervous system. It says, "Pay attention!"

Orbitofrontal Cortex (OFC): Connector

The orbitofrontal cortex (OFC) connects the amygdala (emotional spray-paint) and the prefrontal cortex (bridge of the ship). In other words, it connects feelings with expectancies. Its job is to create an action plan based on past experiences and assess the best path to achieve the goal. *It evaluates the best way to act out your addiction without getting caught.* The OFC engages the prefrontal cortex in planning where, when, and how to better achieve its goals. However, this process of reflection can develop into rumination and preoccupation with addiction.

As Lewis (2015) explains, this is part of how the brain is designed.

> If that reflection turns into rumination, we can't suddenly look for some foreign entity, point our finger, and shout, "Disease!" Rumination is the result of a normal brain, doing what it's designed to do when the brain's owner has entered a cycle of seeking and finding the same thing over and over again. (p. 82)

Interestingly, this is the same process that is involved in love or infatuation as well.

MAKING SENSE OF ADDICTIVE BEHAVIORS

So next time you feel like a moral failure, and you have to take responsibility for hurting yourself and others, remember this: *The adult part of your brain loses connection with the goal-setting part of your brain.*

Your DPC (responsible adult), literally loses connection with your striatum, (motivational engine). Your goals become focused on finding the next dopamine surge as your brain is traveling down the superhighway of dopamine acquisition. Your compassionate self is swept away with gushes of impulsivity and the desperate need to acquire more and more of something that brings you short-term relief and long-term agony.

Now that you are beginning to understand how addiction works in the brain, it will become easier to forgive yourself, and to develop the capacity to sit with the grief that ensues from your actions. This is very important. You cannot heal what you don't feel, and this includes hurting yourself and those you love.

The next practice helps you to explore a time when you lost connection and acted out. Using the ABC model of behavior, it takes you through a process of identifying the antecedent, what came before the acting out, the actual behavior that you engaged in, and the consequences of that behavior. Slowing the process down is hard, but it facilitates your understanding, step by step, of how you did what you did.

> *Practice 11, The ABC Model, can be very helpful for those of you reading along who don't connect with addictive behaviors, but do recognize how you have dissociated and how this numbing behavior has wreaked havoc in your life. You can substitute the word numbing or dissociating for addiction.*

To prepare for Practice 11, in your journal, make three columns on a page. Label the first column **Antecedents**, the second column **Behavior**, and the third column **Consequences**.

Practice 11. Using the ABC Model (Antecedent, Behavior, Consequences)

Gently bring yourself into your quiet, private space, saying hello to your inside self. Begin to notice how it is for you in your body, today, in this moment. Notice what part of your body calls to you, inviting your attention. Notice what state you are in: tense, relaxed, heavy? Invite your grounding felt sense to come into your body.

If you can't find some ventral energy, go to Practice 8, The Felt Sense Polyvagal Grounding Practice, to prepare for Practice 11.

I invite you to find a time where you lost a sense of grounding and acted out your addiction. Perhaps it was a time that you did something that feels so "not you" that it is hard to pause and stay with it. See if you can be gentle with yourself, remembering how the striatum takes over, fueled by dopamine. Let yourself explore the details of the behavior and write them down in the center column of the page.

Pause and connect with your grounded felt sense if you need to.

Then ask yourself: "What were the consequences of that behavior?" Recall how it impacted you and those around you—your family, including partner, children, extended kin, friends, coworkers, community groups, society. Write a detailed description under the consequences column. It is important to take your time and write as much detail as possible. **Remind yourself that when addicted your striatum, your action brain, has lost connection with your responsible adult, the bridge of your ship.** *This will help you to remember more, to be more honest about the damage done, and to have empathy for yourself and those that you hurt.*

Pause. Place a gentle, compassionate hand on your grounded felt sense. You are being brave. It takes courage to delve into this.

Now, drop your attention down inside and ask into your body: "What was happening in my life leading up to this behavior?" Explore the last hours, days, and weeks before. Don't push, just invite your body to recall what events were occurring; let your body sit curiously in the memory part to the felt sense. Remember that nothing has to come into your body now.

When you are ready you can fill in the antecedents column, asking yourself what led up to the behavior. What was happening, or about to happen, before you acted out? Did something trigger you? Maybe an anniversary of something traumatic? Again, be very gentle with yourself as you reflect on how your actions hurt yourself and others.

Now pause and reflect on your ABCs. Notice how you feel in your body now compared to when you started the practice. Perhaps you notice a felt shift?

Make a Process Recording of the experience and/or Body Card.

You can come back to this practice many times, gently inviting a somatic connection. Integrating experiences takes its own time. Our job is to invite the body, not to force anything. With enough safety, comes remembering, mourning, and reconnection.

INTEGRATION

Sometimes this practice leads to profound connections that your body dissociated from to help you survive. The connections can seem obvious once you make them. You may recall an incident of abuse that you disconnected from at the time, but remained in your body, in a dorsal state of numbing. Or a trigger that occurred hours, days, or weeks before that activated the trauma feedback loop. Remember, the body cannot sustain either flight/fight/freeze or fold for too long. It will shift states, activating behaviors that can become addictive.

The next practice integrates all the practices that we have done to date. It brings together neuroception and interoception, helping you to create a behavioral map of your healing journey.

FOUR CIRCLES HARM REDUCTION PRACTICE: A ROADMAP FOR HEALING

Congratulations on arriving at this point in your journey. By now you have become familiar with both skills in the FSPM, recognizing and rewiring neuroception, and Focusing/finding your felt sense. You are ready to delve more deeply.

This practice shapes your treatment plan for harm reduction providing you with specific actions that are neural exercises. People have used it to help with anything from nail biting, lying, substance use, dissociation, compulsive masturbation, cutting the body, etc. The first circle is for addictive behaviors or bad habits that you are ready to modify. The second circle is for triggers that lead you into the first circle behaviors. The third circle is where you place your healthy grounded behaviors that lead to healing. The fourth circle is for behaviors that cultivate deeply spiritual compassionate practices.

Each circle represents a process:

> Inner circle: Letting go
> Second circle: Triggering
> Third circle: Grounding
> Fourth circle: Deepening

I will describe the practice first, and then we can explore how to form FSPM accountability partnerships. It is very important to know that this practice evolves over many months or even years. You build your circles as you build your life.

The Four Circle Harm Reduction Practice (FCHRP) is a tool that I adapted from Patrick Carnes's Three Circle Exercise (2001). The circles provide a map to document your management of addictive or other troublesome behaviors. I integrated the Felt Sense Polyvagal Model into the circles, introducing the ANS states and Focusing practice. You can see that each of the circles includes a 7 F's symbol that signifies what autonomic state the circle represents.

The Four Circles Practice departs from the traditional 12-step model in two ways. Firstly, we are guided by the body. We know from Polyvagal Theory that our body will not shift into a ventral state until it feels safe enough. So, it follows that we need to pay specific attention to neuroception (7 F's) and interoception (felt sense). If the body feels safe enough it will engage in the process of healing. Secondly, the FCHRP uses a harm reduction model which may or may not include sobriety. For example, instead of committing to no alcohol, the sobriety model, you could reduce harm by limiting to two drinks per day. Below is an example of Joe's Four Circle Harm Reduction Plan. Joe and I have been working together on this plan for several years.

See insert after p. 128 for color figure.

THE INNER CIRCLE (FIXATE): LETTING GO

The inner circle represents the blended state of Fixate, where addictive/harmful behaviors live in the ANS. Here is where you put behaviors that you are ready to change. Through your FSPM accountability partnerships you take time to work with your body in deciding what you are ready to let go of or reduce. The behaviors must be quantifiable for clear accountability. In Joe's case, over many months, he committed to no masturbation/watching porn, two desserts a week, and no smoking weed. Most people have several behaviors that they switch up, and they often go together. Joe realized that if he smoked a joint, he was more likely to start watching porn, which led to compulsive masturbation for hours at a time, and then bingeing on sweets. So, to avoid the slippery slope, he was very careful to pay particular attention to stopping marijuana.

As you are considering what to put in your inner circle it is important to make sure that you can track your progress. So, for example, it would be very

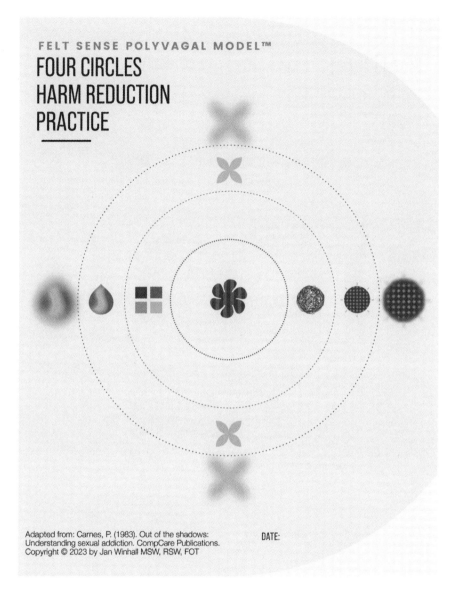

Figure 4.1: Felt Sense Polyvagal Model™ Four Circles Harm Reduction Practice
Source: Copyright © 2021 From *Treating Trauma and Addiction with the Felt Sense Polyvagal Model: A Bottom-Up Approach*, Jan Winhall. Reproduced by permission of Taylor and Francis Group, LLC, a division of Informa plc.

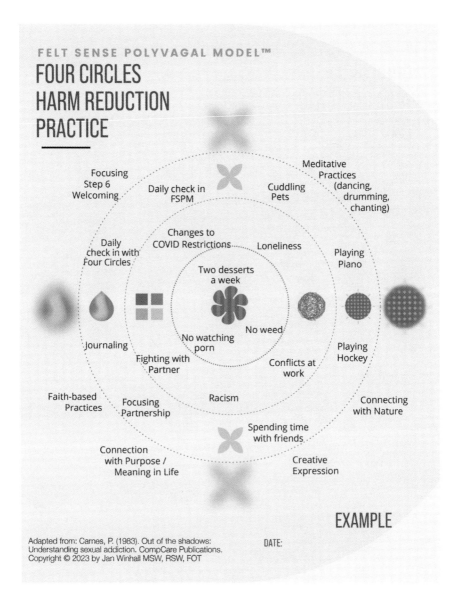

Figure 4.2: Felt Sense Polyvagal Model™ Four Circles Harm Reduction Practice Example

Source: Copyright © 2021 From *Treating Trauma and Addiction with the Felt Sense Polyvagal Model: A Bottom-Up Approach*, Jan Winhall. Reproduced by permission of Taylor and Francis Group, LLC, a division of Informa plc.

difficult to put "No Dissociating" in the inner circle, because it isn't a conscious choice. Instead, as you develop your skill of recognizing and rewiring your ANS state you can *put the behavior that activates the state shift* in the inner circle. In Sue's case, she put "counting" in her inner circle as she gained insight into how that behavior activated a dorsal state of dissociation.

THE SECOND CIRCLE (FIGHT/FLIGHT, FIXATE/FREEZE/ FAWN, FOLD, FAVORING OTHERS FOR SURVIVAL): TRIGGERING

In the second circle are experiences that activate the sympathetic/dorsal branches of the ANS, the trauma feedback loop. Here you list the issues in your life that trigger stressful responses such as job problems, conflicts in relationships, racism, gender discrimination, misogyny, poverty, flashbacks, depression/anxiety. Being specific is helpful. Most people include loneliness in the second circle. As you work with the trauma feedback loop in the 7 F states you are becoming more aware of your triggers. When you list them in the second circle it helps to anticipate and respond to them daily.

THE THIRD CIRCLE (FLOCK, FUN/FIRED UP, FLOWING): GROUNDING

The third circle is the ventral state of health, growth, and restoration. Here you list all of the behaviors that bring a felt sense experience of social connection, intimacy, fun, purpose, and meaning. It takes time to build these, so it isn't uncommon to start with one or two. As you practice them you are inviting more grounding energy into your body. As you feel more grounded you will want to engage in more Flocking activities. One activity reinforces the other, creating new neuropathways of healing. In Joe's case he listed playing hockey with his buddies, Focusing with his FSPM accountability partner, and several other activities.

THE FOURTH CIRCLE (FLOCK, FUN/FIRED UP, FLOWING): DEEPENING

The fourth circle is an extension of the third where deep spiritual practices occur. Here we cultivate an intense connection with self, others, God, and the natural world. Dancing, chanting, singing, praying, writing, playing music, creating, walking in the woods, and spiritual retreats are all practiced in a ventral state. Joe slowly built these practices over several years. Sometimes this state comes in Step 6 of Focusing as you deepen into welcoming a profound felt shift. This would be Level 7 in the experiencing scale.

Let's pause, to take in this large amount of new information. When you are ready you can begin the practice.

In preparation make sure that you and your FSPM partner have a downloaded handout of the Four Circle Harm Reduction Practice and the FSPM 7 F states in front of you along with Body Cards/crayons and a journal.

*Practice 12. Four Circle Harm Reduction Practice

Settle yourself in your chair. Take some time to pause and slowly connect with your inside self. Checking down into the center of your body, begin with Practice 8, Felt Sense Polyvagal Grounding Practice.

Open your eyes, coming back to your quiet space. Begin by looking at your 7 F states. Let your partner know what ANS state you are in.

When ready you can both look at the Four Circles handout. Let your body become familiar with the circles, perhaps discussing them with your partner. There is no right place to start. Let your body be curious, and spend some time noticing what circle draws you in. You can go inside and notice your bodily response.

*You might be drawn to the inner circle, **Letting Go**, ready to commit to changing your problem behaviors. Perhaps you have already tried this many times. Proceed slowly, there is no rush. You need to make sure that you have enough Flock energy to help you follow through. Before you commit, take time to add something to the other circles. You will need this resource to guide you when it gets tough.*

*You might be drawn to the second circle, **Triggering**. Perhaps your triggers feel so intense and overwhelming that you are scared to commit to anything yet. That is just fine. There is time to prepare. Remember, preparation is key to success in changing behaviors. If you feel really stuck here, go to the 5 P's and review. You may need more support to continue.*

*You may be drawn to the third circle, **Grounding**. Some folks feel that they cannot possibly commit to letting go, the inner circle, until they have more good energy, safety, and community in their lives. This is very wise. Building these resources is essential to begin the journey of letting go.*

You may be drawn to the fourth circle, **Deepening**. *Notice what it is that draws you in.*

A word of caution here. If you have a deepening practice such as meditation, or prayer, now is the time to consider whether this practice is grounded in a felt sense. Do you feel whole and integrated when you practice, like Step 6 in Focusing? It is important to assess how integrated you are when engaging in these practices. Sometimes people are dissociating rather than deeply connecting inside. This is sometimes called "spiritual bypassing." You can use your Focusing practice to notice how embodied you feel when deepening. With Focusing we want an alert mind and a relaxed body. If you slip down too deeply becoming sleepy and/or dissociated, you can learn to notice this and come back to presence. Standing up is helpful too.

Take some time to fill in the circles as much or as little as feels right for you. Over time you can discuss how to increase your third and fourth circle, trying out new experiences that bring you into more community.

BEGINNING YOUR FSPM ACCOUNTABILITY PARTNERSHIP

Once you have committed to changing your problem behaviors and have put them in your inner circle, you are ready to add accountability to your Focusing partnership. This means that you will increase your Focusing check-ins to a daily practice with your accountability partner. Remember the plastic paradox. Ruts are hard to get out of. It is possible, but it needs daily attention to form new neuropathways. Neurons that fire together wire together, so each time you check in with your 7 F states and your Four Circles you are rewiring!

You will need to negotiate a new regular daily time to check in. You can continue to do a weekly one-hour time and then add daily 20-minute check-ins. You can also agree to text each other when you feel at risk, recognizing that your partner will get back when possible.

In order to change an inner circle behavior, you need to agree to check first with your accountability partner. For example, over time as you achieve sobriety you may decide to shift behaviors from abstinence to harm reduction. You can then try moving from no alcohol to a limit of 2 drinks a week. It is very important to check this out with your partner first. That way you are making sure that you are changing your behavior based on your dorsolateral prefrontal cortex, your adult responsible self.

HOW TO USE THE FOUR CIRCLES

An Ounce of Prevention: Daily Check-Ins

Morning check-ins are excellent because they can help you organize your day and prevent problems from occurring. For example, you can begin your day by looking at your 7 F states, checking to see what ANS state you are currently in.

Then you look at your Four Circles, starting with the second circle, triggering, and ask yourself, "What is happening today, or around this time in my life that could activate a triggered state?" Take some time to ask inside to your felt sense.

"Oh, yes, there is that issue with my boss. I need to address that today, and I am scared. What can I do to help myself with that anxiety?"

Look at your third and fourth circle behaviors and decide which ones you can do today that will help you. Perhaps you will take some extra time after work to have dinner with your Focusing partner to share how it went. Or you can go to the gym and have a longer sauna afterward. This way you anticipate stressful times and build in extra support. This is an example of living a life with the Bridge of Your Ship in charge. A safe-enough life that you and those you love deserve.

Addictive behaviors are learned habits that attempt to regulate a threatened nervous system caught in a trauma feedback loop (Winhall, 2021). The FSPM invites a new strength-based and empowering definition of addiction that washes away the helplessness and shame. It's important that you have a definition that you can say to yourself and offer to those who are interested in your journey. By their very nature definitions are powerful. They can define us *if we let them*! Maybe you have defined yourself as sick or bad. It's time to let that go.

Try saying this to yourself. "Addiction is a learned habit. It saved me when I felt overwhelmed." The next time someone asks you about addiction, or you hear people talking about it, you might share this simple line. *Addiction is a learned habit. It helped me in the short term, hurt me in the long term, and I couldn't stop.*

SUMMARY

Chapter 4 presents the Felt Sense Polyvagal model of addiction seen through the lens of Marc Lewis's learning model. Current definitions of addictions as sickness or moral failure are replaced with a more sophisticated understanding based on current research in neuroplasticity. Lewis sees addictions as the result of learned, bad habits that are created by trauma feedback loops. An example is presented in a discussion that compares being in love with the state of addiction.

A practice that takes you back to early memories of self-soothing is followed by a description of five main areas of the brain that are involved in addictive behaviors. This knowledge reinforces the understanding that these behaviors are learned habits based on survival strategies, not as brain pathology.

The main practice in the model for working with addiction, called the Four Circle Harm Reduction Practice, is described with an example. Instructions on how to create a FSPM accountability partnership are outlined.

The Underbelly of Addiction: Trauma and Attachment (Practices 13–14)

Chapter 5 takes us into an embodied exploration of trauma, attachment, and addiction. The next five practices (Chapters 5 and 6) explore your life stories, connections between early childhood memories, and subsequent trauma and addictive responses. Remember, everything that you have been working on is preparation for this next part of the journey, and you are not alone in touching into these experiences. Your Felt Sense Polyvagal Model (FSPM) partner/practitioner is there with you. Keep in mind your Five P's as you go through the practices. Pacing is important.

Recall Judith Herman's (1992) three stages of healing: establishing safety, remembering and mourning, and reconnection. So far, we have been working on establishing safety and grounding by creating a safe nest. The FSPM provides a container in which to understand your behavior. As you practice the two skills of recognizing/retuning your ANS (neuroception) and finding your felt sense (interoception) you are establishing safety by building new neuropathways of healing. In creating your Four Circles Harm Reduction Practice you are beginning to incorporate those skills into a plan and a path. Well done! You now have a safe enough container to begin the next stage in healing, wading more deeply into remembering and mourning. As we begin, it will be helpful for you to have a way to assess your experiences of trauma: a way that honors your body's wisdom.

ASSESSING TRAUMA: THE ANS KEEPS THE SCORE

How do you know when you are suffering from trauma? The traditional top-down medical model views trauma through a pathologizing lens. The clinician makes a diagnosis by referring to a list of psychological symptoms in the *Diagnostic and Statistical Manual* (DSM). The diagnosis is based on their impressions of you in the first one or two appointments.

Recently, there has been an increasing acknowledgment of the need to integrate embodiment into trauma assessment and treatment. This is evidenced by the title of trauma expert Bessel van der Kolk's best seller, *The Body Keeps the Score* (2015). Indeed, from a polyvagal lens, this is so true. We can say even more specifically that **the autonomic nervous system keeps the score.**

The Felt Sense Polyvagal Model for assessing trauma is based on the autonomic nervous system, offering a new, embodied paradigm. As you go through the next practices you will be documenting your life journey, uncovering more about your past. You may wonder if you have a significant trauma history. In answering this question, it is helpful to look back at your Process Recordings, particularly Practice 4 (Recognizing/Retuning Your Nervous System States: The 7 F's). Notice where you are in your 7 F states. What states are most common? Most people have a default state or pattern that emerges over time. It is very helpful to document this. For example, many people who are struggling with trauma and addictive patterns can identify the trauma feedback loop of flight/fight/freeze/fawn/fold as their default state.

Let your body be your guide: If you are consistently finding yourself caught in the trauma feedback loop, then you are experiencing significant trauma. Ask yourself what behaviors help you to shift states. Keep on the lookout for addictions. They help your body sustain the trauma feedback loop.

EMBODIED ASSESSMENT AND TREATMENT TOOL (EATT)

For those of you who are practitioners, I created the *Embodied Assessment and Treatment Tool* (Winhall, 2024). This tool, based on the FSPM, enables you to formulate a somatic assessment, document a treatment plan, and store your online clinical notes. It includes both psychological and neurophysiological processes. Instead of focusing on an ever-increasing list of diagnostic categories, you assess peoples' capacity to self-regulate and coregulate their physiological state with others. This is done by tracking each client's nervous system and felt sense.

Many clients also enjoy reviewing the EATT as a way of tracking the process. Looking back helps to reflect on the journey, to recall resources that were helpful, and to construct a cohesive narrative over time.

AM I TOO SENSITIVE? AM I MAKING IT UP?

"According to the FSPM I am living my life in the trauma feedback loop, but I don't have any trauma history. My parents are good, loving people. My siblings are fine. I didn't experience horrible events that are defined as traumatic. My problem is me, I'm just too sensitive."

Do you ever feel like you are causing your own problems? Have you been told that you are exaggerating? Or people look at you suspiciously when you try to describe how anxious, or frustrated you are? Feeling blamed and misunderstood fuels suffering. One of many problems with the traditional top-down approach to treating trauma is that it is defined by a list of events that happened to you. This results in people feeling invalidated if they cannot find any event to identify with. "Well, nothing on that list fits for me, so I must be crazy."

No, you are not crazy. Your body is telling you something loud and clear. Your autonomic nervous system is picking up threat. You cannot argue with that, neuroception is an unconscious process. The answer lies in shifting the paradigm away from defining trauma simply by external events. Instead, we focus on listening to how each person is carrying their embodied experience of life. Gabor Maté puts it like this:

> Trauma/injury is about what happens *inside* us, and how those effects persist, not what happens *to* us. An inquiry into "Why the pain?" has to leave space for the kinds of emotional injuries that may elude conscious recall or, much more often, seem unremarkable to the person doing the remembering. (Maté, 2022, p. 226)

It is quite possible to have experienced loving and kind parents who were not able to attune to your needs. This lack of attunement may have led to your feeling abandoned, disconnected, or under threat. Maybe your folks didn't understand you, or they were not able to give you what they knew you needed, or they were preoccupied with providing food and shelter for the family. This can be traumatic. Or maybe your parents gave you a safe nest, but the culture that you live in did not accept you. This is also traumatic, and often invisible to an undiscerning eye. There is much that our society has silenced, denied, mislabeled, and pathologized. If your suffering is not recognized by your family and/or culture, then you will feel invalidated and unsupported. You will be marginalized.

Let's pause here and take time to reflect on how you relate to your suffering. Can you identify the feelings that underlie your trauma? Notice how your body responds to the question. Where are you in your nervous system? Remember that what may be traumatic for one person is not necessarily traumatic for another. Not every soldier returning from war will stay stuck in the trauma feedback loop. *Each body responds uniquely and must be honored as such.*

AN ANTI-OPPRESSIVE LENS

> *To hold traumatic reality in consciousness requires a social context that affirms and protects the victim and that joins victim and witness in a common alliance.*
> —HERMAN, 1992, P. 19

Herman speaks of the need to create a welcoming space, so that people will feel safe enough to speak of experiences that have felt unspeakable. When we don't feel safe to speak, we become silenced in a way that isolates us. For too long our culture has silenced those who have suffered from trauma/addiction. Silencing is a form of oppression: an attempt to "push down" whatever threatens the status quo. The Felt Sense Polyvagal Model embraces an antioppressive lens, supporting a social movement of liberation for all peoples.

> The drug addict is today's scapegoat. Viewed honestly, much of our culture is geared towards enticing us away from ourselves, into externally directed activity, into diverting the mind from ennui and distress. The hardcore addict surrenders her pretense about that. Her life is all about escape. The rest of us can, with varying success, maintain our charade, but to do so, we banish her to the margins of society. (Maté, 2010, p. 266)

What does it mean to be banished to the margins of society? To be marginalized is to be oppressed, to be held down, and pushed aside. Iris Young, a professor of political science at the University of Chicago back in the 1990s, developed a sophisticated body of work related to the systemic nature of oppression. Young helped us to understand how it shows up in political, legal, economic, and cultural institutions.

MICRO AND MACRO AGGRESSIONS

Young (1998) studied both macro and micro aggressions in her research. Macro aggressions are the most common ways of understanding oppression. Examples include things like unequal pay structures or acts of racism against a group. Micro-aggressions are much more subtle. Well-meaning people can perpetuate oppression unconsciously. For example, sexist remarks or racial stereotyping can often occur without acknowledgment. Young devoted much of her work to studying the intersection of micro and macro aggressions by emphasizing the hidden nature of oppression. Her work helped us to see how complex our social identity can be.

It gets complicated when we recognize that we can be members of both oppressed and privileged groups. Freeing ourselves from being oppressed also means becoming aware of how we may be part of a group that has a history of oppressing. For example, I belong to a very privileged white, upper-middle-class professional group, and as a woman, I belong to an oppressed female group subjected to systemic misogyny.

I grew up in Canada in a white, heteronormative, Christian, nuclear family–based culture. Even so, my family was oppressed by the prevailing cultural norms and values. My parents divorced at a time when divorce was rare. My father left the family. My mother was hospitalized for several years. My family history includes addiction, depression, and parental suicide attempts. As a child, I looked around for other families that looked like mine, but there were none to be found. All of this led to me feeling marginalized and ashamed.

Where are you in the intersection of trauma, oppression, and addiction? These are big questions that we will continue to explore. For now, let's start by noticing what groups you identify with, and your experiences of privilege and oppression. Practice 13, The Wheel of Privilege, helps you to become familiar with your social identity, the part of yourself that is defined by the groups that you belong to. Social identity theory was formulated by Henri Tajfel and John Turner in the 1970s (Tajfel & Turner, 1985). This theory helps you assess how these groups intersect with your power and privilege. An example of a group would be one based on race or gender.

THE WHEEL OF PRIVILEGE

The Wheel of Privilege (2023) was created as a way to visually guide you in understanding your position in terms of power and privilege. The wheel shows how your position intersects with others in our society. There are several versions of the wheel. I chose this one because it includes many different groups and emphasizes those whose marginalization may be hidden. As you see from my example, we can be part of several disparate groups.

The wheel divides the spectrum of power and privilege into three rings. The inner ring is the **Power** group. Here we find the groups that hold the most privilege in our society, for example, a white cisgendered male. The second circle are the **Erased** group. This refers to those whose marginalization is hidden, minimized, or dismissed. An example of this would be those who are BIPOC and present as white, those who are invisibly disabled, or those who learned English as a second language. The outer ring is the **Marginalized** group, referring to those who have the least privilege in our society. Examples include folks who are visibly gender nonconforming, visibly BIPOC, poor, homeless, or prisoners.

*Practice 13. The Wheel of Privilege

Settle into your private space. Take some time to familiarize yourself with the Wheel of Privilege (https://just1voice.com/advocacy/wheel-of-privilege). You may come back to it several times as you think about your experiences. After you finish the practice, you take turns Focusing with your partner, deepening your understanding of your social identity and how it has impacted you. No doubt, some of you will be very aware of your social position. For others it is a very eye-opening experience. If you find yourself in marginalized groups, it can be validating to appreciate that much has been against you, helping you to be more compassionate with yourself. If you identify with more privileged groups, it can challenge you to reflect on how this has impacted you and your life story.

CHILDHOOD TRAUMA: THE UNDERBELLY OF ADDICTION

Gabor Maté is adamant in his belief that trauma underlies all addictive behavior. This makes sense if we think of trauma as a state in the autonomic nervous system that forms a feedback loop, and addictions being trauma state regulation strategies within that autonomic loop. While Maté acknowledges there may be some collection of genes that predispose people to susceptibility, this is not the same as saying that addiction is predetermined. Genes are turned on and off by the environment, and early adversity affects genetic activity in ways that set the stage for future problems. Maté points out that research with both humans and animals confirms that any genetic risks for substance abuse can be mitigated by a safe and nurturing home (Mate, 2022, p. 230).

Maté is clear in saying that addictions can be best understood as "a natural response to unnatural circumstances, an attempt to soothe the pain of injuries incurred in childhood and stresses sustained in adulthood" (Mate, 2022, p. 216). Notice how well this definition fits with my statement that addictions are adaptive (natural) responses to (unnatural) maladaptive environments. In stressing the environmental causes, we are drawn back to childhood experiences. To what extent are these early experiences the root cause of addictions? To explore the answer to this compelling and controversial question we turn to the extensive research done by Vincent Felitti.

FELITTI'S ADVERSE CHILDHOOD EXPERIENCES SCALE (ACES)

The adverse childhood experiences scale (ACES) was part of the most well-known study to date on the relationship between trauma and addiction. Felitti (1998) conducted the research between 1995 and 1997. He became interested in this work through a relationship that he had with a patient he calls Patty (Felitti, 2016). As you read about their journey together, notice how he allows himself to be open and curious, and above all, committed to listening to Patty's reality. Some of you will find yourselves in her story.

During the 1980s Felitti was running a weight loss program in the Kaiser Permanente Department of Preventive Medicine in San Diego. It became apparent that patients who were losing weight were the most likely to drop out of the program. This disturbed Felitti, prompting him to interview 286 people who had left the program. To his surprise, he discovered that the majority of them had been sexually abused as children (Felitti, 2002).

Patty's story impressed Felitti (2016). At the time that they met, she was 28 years old, working as a nursing aide at a seniors' home. She entered the program weighing 408 pounds. At the end of 51 weeks of a fasting regimen she weighed 132 pounds. A success story, right?

Patty maintained the weight for several weeks but soon gained back 37 pounds. Felitti asked himself how it was possible to gain this much weight in three weeks. As he explored more with Patty, she told him that when she was a child she used to sleepwalk. In recent weeks she was waking in the morning to find her kitchen in a big mess. It was full of pots and pans and stale food. She assumed that she must have been sleepwalking and cooking food in the middle of the night.

Felitti was determined to solve this mystery and describes how he asked Patty many times why she thought she was gaining weight at this point. Eventually she shared that recently a married fellow at work had told her that she was attractive and suggested that they go on a date. Felitti understood that this was not a good situation, but he kept inviting Patty to share more about why she thought this would provoke such an intense response. Eventually she shared that her grandfather had sexually abused her for years when she was a child. It simply wasn't safe to be seen as attractive. Soon after this Patty withdrew from the program, no doubt feeling overwhelmed by the traumatic feelings that resurfaced with the disclosure. Unfortunately, Felitti lost touch with her.

Twelve years later, she returned to the clinic weighing over 400 pounds again. In the meantime, Felitti had started a separate group for patients that weighed 400 to 600 pounds and hadn't been able to lose weight in the program. He formed this group to help him answer the question, "What is the engine underneath eating yourself to death?"

Patty joined the group, sharing that several years ago she had bariatric surgery and lost 94 pounds. After that she became suicidal, resulting in five hospitalizations and three rounds of electroshock therapy. When Felitti interviewed Patty this time she said that as the weight was coming off, she felt that her "wall was coming down" too fast. She became frightened of becoming attractive and losing the protective barrier, so she shut down and went back to binge eating. Making the connection between the sexual abuse and her binge eating was too much for her nervous system to support. Unfortunately she shut down, again shifting into a dorsal state.

This pattern may be familiar to you. There may have been times when you touched into a traumatic memory and then returned to a dissociative state because it was too overwhelming. This is a common response. The body is slowly titrating the trauma, touching into it and then distancing. It's important to notice this pattern and reflect. You have an opportunity now to stay the course. You have your focusing partner and your therapist to coregulate your journey as you engage in the 20 embodied practices.

FELITTI'S PARADIGM SHIFT: THE CONTEXT TELLS THE STORY

Felitti realized that what he had perceived to be the problem, Patty perceived to be the solution.

This was a key point in the development of his research. He realized that he had been on the right track in listening to Patty, encouraging her to share her feelings and traumatic experiences. This led to her develop insight into her behavior. As she explored her feelings it became clear that she needed to gain weight in order to keep herself safe from being the target of a man's sexual attention. Then it all began to make sense. In the context of Patty's trauma history being sexually attractive was unsafe, so she unconsciously returned to eating to hide. This addictive behavior also perpetuated the trauma feedback loop, facilitating a dorsal numbing state. This was Patty's way of soothing overwhelming feelings. Felitti (2019) realized that gaining weight was Patty's solution. He was struck by the power of listening to his patients. He says this very clearly: "We listened. Period."

Patty's story is a good example of how important it is to understand behavior through the lens of the autonomic nervous system. When Felitti tried to understand from a top-down pathologizing lens, the weight gain made no sense. In fact, it seemed masochistic. But when he listened to Patty's own bodily knowing, he understood her embodied response for what it was, an attempt to stay safe. In the context of Patty's sexual abuse history, weight gain was a survival strategy.

Understanding the context in which your trauma responses developed is key to healing. **The context tells the story of your wound**. It frees you from shame when you realize that your body's wisdom helped you to survive. You, like Patty, are not weird or crazy. We will dig into this in the next practice. First, a discussion of some results of Felitti's research.

FELITTI'S FINDINGS

In 2004, Felitti published his findings in a now well-known study that demonstrated the strong link between childhood adversity and chronic health problems. This study has had a huge impact in the fields of trauma, addiction, and preventative medicine. The study was done within a single health care system in San Diego with a sample size of over 17,000 middle class American adults. The group was 80% white, 10% Black, and 10% Asian; 74% had gone to college; 49% were men; and the mean age was 57.

The study included eight categories of adverse childhood experiences (ACEs):

> Recurrent and severe physical abuse (11%)
> Recurrent and severe emotional abuse (11%)
> Contact sexual abuse (women 28%, men 16%)
> Growing up in a household with:
> An alcoholic or drug user (25%)
> A household member being imprisoned (3%)
> A mentally ill, chronically depressed, or institutionalized household
> member (19%)
> A mother being treated violently (12%)
> Both biological parents absent (22%)

Participants scored one point for each category that was relevant. An ACE score could range from zero to eight. Felitti (2004) reported that a person with an ACE score of 6 is 2.5 times more likely to be a smoker and six times more likely to be addicted to alcohol than a child whose ACE score is 0. Injection of street drugs also increases dramatically and in direct correlation with increases in ACE score. *A male child with an ACE score of 6, compared to a male child with an ACE score of 0, has a 4,600 percent increase in the likelihood of injecting drugs.*

Felitti (2004) came to a powerful conclusion after reviewing his research into the impact of early adverse experiences:

> Our findings are disturbing to some because they imply that the basic causes of
> addiction lie within us and the way we treat each other, not in drug dealers or

dangerous chemicals. They suggest that billions of dollars have been spent every-where except where the answer is to be found. (p. 3)

Felitti disagrees with the current brain disease model of addiction. Instead he suggests a psychodynamic interpretation, looking at underlying psychological factors that are the result of trauma. He states that addiction involves:

> unconscious although understandable decisions being made to seek chemical relief from the ongoing effects of old trauma, often at the cost of accepting future health risks. Expressions like "self-destructive behavior" are misleading and should be dropped because . . . they overlook the importance of the obvious short-term benefits that drive the use of these substances. (2004, p. 8)

Felitti says "unconscious although understandable" decisions are being made to act out addictive behaviors. This view is compatible with the Felt Sense Polyvagal Model: the unconscious, autonomic response of the nervous system seeks survival. Felitti also refers to the term "self-destructive" as inaccurate, thus advocating for a nonpathologizing model. Again, he stresses that the context tells the story (Felitti, 2004). We have much to be thankful for in Felitti's contribution. His wisdom in listening to his patients has contributed to foundational work in understanding the systemic issues that underlie trauma and addiction. Let's pause and take this in.

LATER ACES STUDIES

The first ACES study was overrepresented by white, middle-class people. Melissa Merrick (2018) conducted the next and largest study with a more diverse group. Merrick's sample included 214,157 people living in 23 states in the U.S. from 2011 to 2014. This study asked similar questions to the first one with one significant addition. They added parental separation or divorce to the list. The link between trauma, addiction, and oppression deepens with Merrick's (2018) results. This is a very important finding in understanding how systems of oppression are precursors to trauma and addiction responses. Reflect on your Wheel of Privilege as you read the results of the study.

Here are Merrick's findings (2018):

1. Those who identified as Black or Latino, with less than a high school education, or annual income lower than $15,000 were more likely to have higher ACE scores.
2. Multiracial, gay, lesbian, and bisexual people were the highest-scoring groups. Multiracial participants scored average of 2.5 ACES, and bisexual adults scored 3.1.
3. Women, younger adults, unemployed people, and those unable to work also scored higher.

Pause here and ask yourself what these results tell us. If you are part of an oppressed group your chances of being traumatized increase significantly. This leads to a much higher chance of experiencing physical and emotional problems, abuse, and addiction.

WHAT IS YOUR ACES SCORE?

Understanding how your social identity impacts your trauma history is an important part of making sense of your behavior. Are you ready to calculate your score? Let's pause and return to Felitti's eight categories. Now add the one that Merrick suggested, parental separation or divorce. Out of the list of nine categories, give yourself one point for each category that applies to you. The total of points is your individual ACEs score.

As you are reflecting on your score it is important to remember two important points that we have discussed. First, many experiences such as community violence, racism, and other forms of oppression, natural disasters, and housing insecurity are not asked about. This means that many additional stressful situations are not taken into account. Second, everyone is unique, and adverse childhood experiences will affect each person differently. For some folks, challenges appear to be "water off a duck's back." Or we might say that they are "thick-skinned." For others the opposite is true. They are delicate and what is now termed "highly sensitive." It follows that a low score doesn't necessarily mean that you didn't suffer from trauma. Equally, a high score doesn't necessarily mean that you will be at risk.

In addition, the exercise fails to ask if you had some mitigating factors that helped you to build resilience, such as a stable and supportive relationship with an adult. It is hopeful to realize that people with high levels of adverse childhood

Item	
Recurrent and severe physical abuse	
Recurrent and severe emotional abuse	
Contact sexual abuse	
Growing up in a household with an alcoholic or a drug user	
Growing up in a household with a member being imprisoned	
Growing up in a household with a mentally ill, chronically depressed, or institutionalized member	
Growing up in a household with a mother being treated violently	
Growing up in a household with both biological parents absent	
Parental separation or divorce	
TOTAL SCORE	

experiences can and do overcome adversity. You are in this process right now, building a new life, creating new healthy neuropathways.

ATTACHMENT THEORY: HOLDING AND LETTING GO

Now we will turn to the field of attachment theory to help us explore the link between childhood adversity and the development of trauma and addictions. In Chapter 1 we discussed the five theories that form the theoretical framework for the Felt Sense Polyvagal Model: Feminist Theory, Focusing, Trauma Theory, Interpersonal Neurobiology (IPNB), and Polyvagal Theory.

Dan Siegel's theory of interpersonal neurobiology developed as a result of his experience as a psychiatrist in training. He was deeply disturbed by the lack of interpersonal connection between physicians and their patients. This lack of empathy led him on a journey to integrate presence of "mind" in his way of relating to his patients. He coined the term "mindsight" to describe this ability to perceive the internal world of self and others. In other words, to be able to appreciate and connect with our inner world and those we are relating to (2012, p. A1-52). He felt that once we become aware of another person's inner world, we can connect in a felt sense way. This is what he believed was missing in medical training and practice.

The concept of mindsight is central in the development of IPNB and has provided a new paradigm in psychotherapy. This model integrates the neuro-biological and interpersonal realms, teaching clients how to manage emotional regulation through neural exercises. Siegel created a meditation tool called The Wheel of Awareness that helps clients learn how to self-regulate and achieve ventral states of integration (2010b, p. 94).

Attachment theory is a central framework in IPNB. Originally postulated by John Bowlby (1969), and Mary Ainsworth (2015), the theory claims that *early relationships with our primary caretakers shape our capacity to self-regulate*. The attachment system is innate in mammals. It motivates us to be close to our care-givers, particularly when we feel under threat. How our caregivers respond to our needs shapes our sense of safety and trust. So, if you experienced a high degree of adverse childhood experiences it makes sense that it would be difficult to form trusting relationships throughout your life. Trusting relationships shape your sense of self as a grounded person. Without trusting relationships, it is difficult to emotionally and neurophysiologically regulate yourself.

Knowing this can help you understand why establishing safe relationships can be so confusing and very difficult. Many of you will have struggled with relationships. It is not because you are incompetent or defective. We all need to feel a consistent source of safety and trust to develop the capacity to create healthy relationships. Be gentle with yourself here.

Attachment theory tells us that your autonomic nervous system needs the warmth of social engagement to feel safe to settle into the sweet spot of ventral energy. In the absence of safe secure attachment, the body shifts into the trauma feedback loop to survive. If you are living in the trauma feedback loop much of the time the good news is that you can develop a secure attachment with yourself and others through neural exercises such as mindsight and the twenty practices that you are engaged in now.

There are two broad categories of attachment: secure/insecure and organized/disorganized. Secure describes a "good enough" level of emotional and physical safety for the child to thrive. Organized attachment patterns lead to a healthy developing brain, and the capacity to formulate a coherent life story. It is important to recognize that we have different attachment styles for each relationship. It may be that you have a secure attachment with your mother and an insecure/avoid-ant attachment with your father. Because the theory is based on white-bodied, nuclear family culture, you may have to adjust to your own family constellation.

An important point to note is that one needs to be very careful in assessing early attachment patterns when working with addiction. It is a complex issue that is highly impacted by cultural norms. Sometimes it involves early history, and sometimes not. It may be that a growing number of people are developing addiction in adolescence and adulthood due to the highly addictive nature of our dislocated society. Bruce Alexander writes extensively about the impact of our culture's social isolation (2008).

CLASSIFICATIONS OF ATTACHMENT

Bowlby's early ideas about the power of secure attachment relationships was tested by his colleague Mary Ainsworth. She conducted research using the *strange situation procedure* (Ainsworth, Behar, Waters, & Wall, 2015). The SSP is a laboratory-based research method for measuring infants' attachment styles based on their reaction to being separated from their primary caretakers.

Ainsworth created eight three-minute segments where the mother either leaves her baby alone in a room, or with a stranger. The study is designed to observe how the baby responds in both of these situations. From this research Ainsworth created three attachment styles: secure, insecure/ambivalent, and insecure/avoidant. A fourth attachment style, disorganized, was subsequently defined by Main and Solomon (1990).

From a FSPM perspective it is helpful to think of these different attachment styles in terms of our embodied sense of being connected to our primary care-takers. *As we go through each style you can imagine how it feels in your body, being curious about which attachment style reflects your relationship with each of your parents. Were you held safely, or with too much distance?*

> *Secure*: safely held in loving arms. Secure attachment holds baby
>   with the right amount of closeness and distance. The caregiver(s)
>   lean in when baby needs comforting, and lean out, easing the
>   hold, as baby moves into the world. Baby feels valued, under-
>   stood, and loved. Baby's body relaxes, nuzzling in and trusting
>   the safety of a warm embrace.
> *Insecure-Avoidant*: unsafely held with distance. The avoidant care-
>   giver(s) withhold from baby, creating a sense of unease. The little
>   body learns to be cautious, sensing the low level of caregiver

presence. Baby feels rejected, held too far away. Baby's body remains vigilant and craving comfort.

Insecure-Ambivalent: Unpredictably held, too close and too far away. Ambivalent caregivers are unpredictable in their capacity to respond to baby's needs. If they do respond they may hold baby too close, in a suffocating way, sometimes projecting their own needs onto them. At other times they are avoidant, turning away from their baby's needs. The inconsistency is confusing, resulting in an anxious, hyperaroused bodily state. Trust cannot be established because of the chaotic responses of the caregiver.

Disorganized: Not safe, not held enough. Disorganized attachment is the most distressing and damaging relationship for baby. Caregivers in this pattern are either terrified and shut down in a dissociative state, or they are abusive and terrifying to baby. Either way, they are not available to see or respond to baby's needs in a predictable and safe way. Baby is unprotected, living in an unresolvable paradox: The caregiver who is supposed to be the source of comfort, becomes the source of their distress. Unable to resolve this dilemma, baby will first become anxious, and eventually give up, shutting down into a collapsed, trancelike state of defeat. This attachment style often leads to addictions as baby grows up, shaped by an endless trauma feedback loop. *Interestingly, this unresolvable dilemma is mirrored in the state of addiction. "What helps you, then harms you."*

Pause here and let your body take in the four attachment styles.

MAPPING ATTACHMENT STYLES AND THE FELT SENSE POLYVAGAL MODEL

Now we can begin to integrate Siegel's work with interpersonal neurobiology and attachment styles into our FSPM. He asks us to think of each attachment style in terms of what autonomic states are involved. Looking at the FSPM clinician version, you can see how secure attachment is present in the ventral state of Flock. We need the presence of ventral energy to feel safe and securely attached.

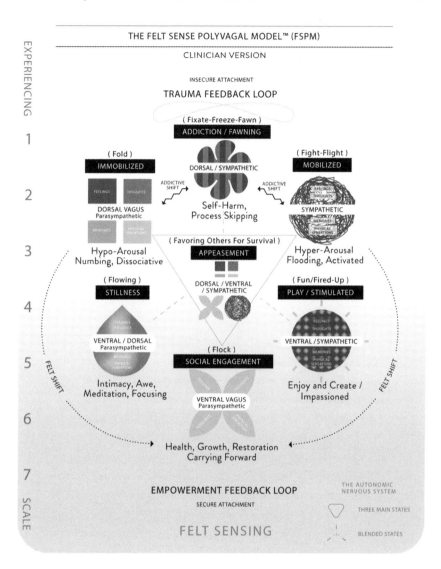

Figure 2.2: The Felt Sense Polyvagal Model™ (FSPM) Clinician Version
Source: Copyright © 2021 From *Treating Trauma and Addiction with the Felt Sense Polyvagal Model: A Bottom-Up Approach,* Jan Winhall. Reproduced by permission of Taylor and Francis Group, LLC, a division of Informa plc.

Flock: *Secure Attachment.* The ventral vagal state of integration depicted at the bottom of the model.

Flight/Fight: *Insecure Avoidant/Ambivalent Attachment.* On the right is the sympathetic state of chaos.

Fold: *Insecure/Disorganized Attachment.* On the left is the dorsal vagal state of rigidity. This is the state of serious threat.

Blended States

Fun/Fired Up: *Secure Attachment.* This blended state is regulated by the ventral branch of the vagus, creating a secure connection. While it is blended with the sympathetic branch and therefore an activated state, it maintains a sense of grounding and safety. Baby embodies a relaxed state with some sympathetic excitement: laughter, eyes bright and curious, arms and legs kicking in a playful way.

Flowing: *Secure Attachment.* This blended state is regulated by the ventral branch of the vagus and therefore enables a secure attachment. Because it is blended with the dorsal branch of the vagus, it sustains a sense of safety. Baby feels relaxed, safe in the stillness, enjoying the closeness of being breastfed, or gazing, being rocked, or being cradled.

Fold/Fawn/Fixate/Freeze/Flight/Fight: *Insecure/Disorganized Attachment.* The blending of the sympathetic and dorsal branches of the autonomic nervous system, known as the Trauma Feedback Loop. The absence of enough safety prevents ventral energy. The ACEs study demonstrated that those who are raised in this state will be more likely to develop addictions (Felitti, 2004).

Favoring Others for Survival: *Insecure attachment.* This is a blending of sympathetic, ventral, and dorsal autonomic states. This kind of appeasing behavior is shaped over time by the caregiver's lack of nurturing response to the child's needs. In the absence of enough coregulation the child learns to be subservient. Serving the caregivers needs becomes a way of surviving. The body will be oscillating between sympathetic constriction, to shutting down in a dorsal slump, with some periods of ventral energy.

CRITIQUING ATTACHMENT THEORY

It is important to bring an anti-oppressive lens to the field of attachment theory. We noted that the first ACE studies (1998, 2004) were based on white culture, missing many experiences of marginalized groups. This is also true for attachment theory. While the first studies were conducted in Uganda by Mary Ainsworth (1967), they were found to be difficult to conduct and moved into a laboratory in the United States. The reason they were difficult to conduct illustrates the critique of the theory. Ainsworth designed a study based on how children respond to their mothers in stressful situations to evaluate how secure an attachment they had formed. But in Uganda families are not based on the nuclear model. In fact, children have several mothers as their primary caregivers. So, when Ainsworth was trying to assess how children were responding to one mother, in their natural environment (not a laboratory) another mother who would be close by would distract and potentially soothe the baby, thus making it impossible to control the variables. This illustrates how much we miss when white culture permeates our thinking, our development of theory, and treatment strategies.

Increasingly there is an awareness that other cultures create secure attachment to land, ancestors, rituals, food, spirit, the body, or any living being or process that creates a feeling of safety and connection. Recall the example of the Mi'kmaw, who associate mother, Earth, and the heartbeat of the drum to evoke feelings of safety and connection. As you go through the classifications, I encourage you to reflect on your culture, bringing an open-minded perspective to your personal journey. Who were your caretakers? Was there a primary caretaker? How does your culture care for their children? What soothed you—a person, a place, a pet, or part of the natural world? Or maybe you created a rich fantasy land. Some children find comfort in a blanket, a toy, something that feels soft, or makes a soothing sound. Use your senses to ask your body how it seeks comfort and safety.

Practice 14 is similar to Practice 10 (First Memories of Feeling Soothed) but this time we will go deeper into a childhood wound, noticing what soothed you when you were small. Then we compare that to what soothes you now as an adult. While you may do some of the practices alone sometimes, it is important to do this practice with your FSPM partner and/or therapist. Check in with your FSPM Focusing partner to make sure they feel coregulated with you as you begin.

*Practice 14. Attachment Exercise: Healing Early Wounds

Bring yourself into your quiet, private space, slowly beginning to settle inside. Take time to clear space if you need to. I invite you to find some grounding energy in your body, and gently place your hand there to anchor you. Feeling your feet on the floor, breathing down into the center of your body. Pause here and let a handle come for the felt sense of feeling connected. If you cannot find grounding now, go back to a beginning practice, resource a body card for ventral energy, or take a break and go for a walk. Remember, do not engage in this or any practice that takes you into uncomfortable feelings unless you are grounded in some flock energy in your body.

Ask your body to find a time when you were a child, when you felt sad, lonely, angry, lost, deeply wounded, a time when you felt overwhelmed with pain. Remember to be beside it, not to fall into it. You and your partner are here together keeping this part of you company. Take your time to get the right distance from the wound. You can back up from it by taking some breaths and placing it miles away from you, or on a movie screen. Then you can bring it closer incrementally as you feel into the felt sense of grounding.

Feel into your hand resting on the grounded place. Ask your body where you feel the wounded place. If you can find it, gently place your hand there. If not, that is fine. It will come when your nervous system feels safe enough to feel it in your body. You will do this practice many times in your healing journey, as you touch into wounded places.

Notice where you are. What is the story of your wound?

> *Who is there?*
> *How old are you?*
> *Where did you go for comfort as a child?*
> *What did you need that you didn't get?*
> *Where do you go now for comfort as an adult? What soothes you now?*
> *Notice, are the ways you soothe yourself now similar or different than when you were a child?*

Pause and let your child part know they are not alone. You are here now with your partner/therapist in the wounded place. You are learning how to listen to your pain. Let this small part of you know that you will return to be with them, to bring comfort and safety to this special part of you. Pause, and when you are ready slowly bring attention back to your feet on the floor, your back supported by the chair.

In your Process Recording ask yourself:

7 F's

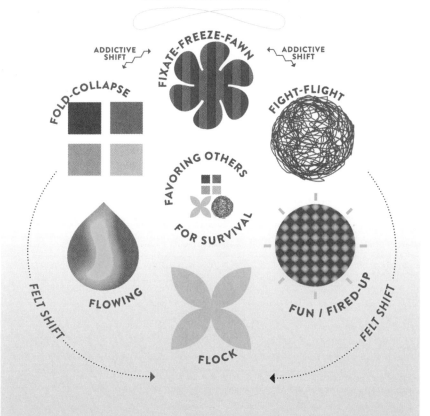

TRAUMA FEEDBACK LOOP

ADDICTIVE SHIFT

FIXATE-FREEZE-FAWN

ADDICTIVE SHIFT

FOLD-COLLAPSE

FIGHT-FLIGHT

FAVORING OTHERS FOR SURVIVAL

FELT SHIFT

FLOWING

FLOCK

FUN / FIRED-UP

FELT SHIFT

EMPOWERMENT FEEDBACK LOOP

FELT SENSING

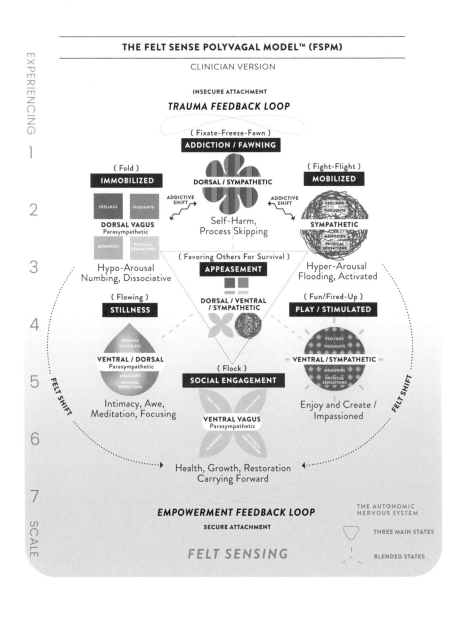

THE FELT SENSE POLYVAGAL MODEL™ (FSPM)

CLINICIAN VERSION

INSECURE ATTACHMENT

TRAUMA FEEDBACK LOOP

(Fixate-Freeze-Fawn)

ADDICTION / FAWNING

(Fold)

IMMOBILIZED

DORSAL / SYMPATHETIC

ADDICTIVE SHIFT

(Fight-Flight)

MOBILIZED

FEELINGS   THOUGHTS

ADDICTIVE SHIFT

FEELINGS THOUGHTS

DORSAL VAGUS
Parasympathetic

MEMORIES   PHYSICAL SENSATIONS

Self-Harm,
Process Skipping

SYMPATHETIC

MEMORIES PHYSICAL SENSATIONS

(Favoring Others For Survival)

Hypo-Arousal
Numbing, Dissociative

APPEASEMENT

Hyper-Arousal
Flooding, Activated

(Flowing)

STILLNESS

DORSAL / VENTRAL / SYMPATHETIC

(Fun/Fired-Up)

PLAY / STIMULATED

FEELINGS THOUGHTS

VENTRAL / DORSAL
Parasympathetic

MEMORIES PHYSICAL SENSATIONS

(Flock)

SOCIAL ENGAGEMENT

FEELINGS THOUGHTS

VENTRAL / SYMPATHETIC

MEMORIES PHYSICAL SENSATIONS

Intimacy, Awe,
Meditation, Focusing

FEELINGS THOUGHTS

VENTRAL VAGUS
Parasympathetic

MEMORIES PHYSICAL SENSATIONS

Enjoy and Create /
Impassioned

FELT SHIFT

FELT SHIFT

Health, Growth, Restoration
Carrying Forward

EMPOWERMENT FEEDBACK LOOP

SECURE ATTACHMENT

FELT SENSING

THE AUTONOMIC
NERVOUS SYSTEM

THREE MAIN STATES

BLENDED STATES

EXPERIENCING

1

2

3

4

5

6

7

SCALE

FELT SENSE POLYVAGAL MODEL™

FOUR CIRCLES
HARM REDUCTION
PRACTICE

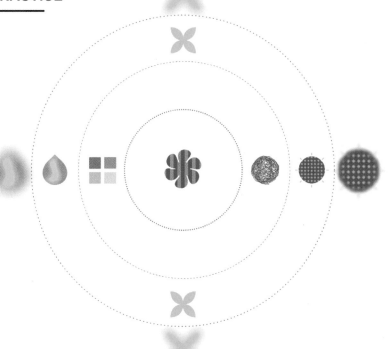

DATE:

FOUR CIRCLES
HARM REDUCTION
PRACTICE

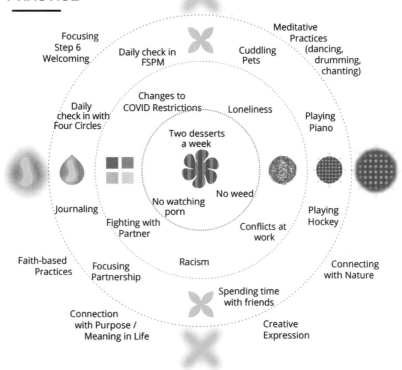

Focusing
Step 6
Welcoming

Daily check in
FSPM

Cuddling
Pets

Meditative
Practices
(dancing,
drumming,
chanting)

Changes to
COVID Restrictions

Loneliness

Daily
check in with
Four Circles

Playing
Piano

Two desserts
a week

No watching
porn

No weed

Journaling

Playing
Hockey

Fighting with
Partner

Conflicts at
work

Faith-based
Practices

Focusing
Partnership

Racism

Connecting
with Nature

Connection
with Purpose /
Meaning in Life

Spending time
with friends

Creative
Expression

EXAMPLE

DATE:

Adapted from: Carnes, P. (1983). Out of the shadows:
Understanding sexual addiction. CompCare Publications.
Copyright © 2023 by Jan Winhall MSW, RSW, FOT

A. *Notice where you are in your 7 states. Has your body shifted in any way? Perhaps you feel a loosening, a felt shift that comes with feeling into the wounded place. What is this shift all about?*

B. *Or you may feel a sense of uneasiness. If so, take your time and ask your partner to help you find your handle for grounded energy. You may want to look at a ventral Body Card.*

C. *What attachment style do you identify with? Are your attachment styles the same or different with different caregivers? Are they part of the trauma feedback loop?*

D. *Is your comforting behavior the same or different than when you were a child?*

With time and practice your body will be able to feel grounded and wounded at the same time. Invite your grounded place to make a caring relationship with your wounded place. Notice how it feels to be connected to the healing energy of the grounded place. Follow your body's wisdom in showing you how to comfort your wounded place.

Make a Process Recording and/or Body Card.

SUMMARY

Chapter 5 brings you into Judith Herman's second stage of healing, remembering and mourning, by exploring the relationship between trauma, attachment and addiction. Ways of assessing severity of trauma are discussed including a presentation of the Embodied Assessment and Treatment Tool.

The Wheel of Privilege helps assess social location as a factor in the development of trauma and addiction. Felitti's research in the Adverse Childhood Experiences Scale (ACES) provides empirical evidence for the link between early trauma, insecure attachment, and the subsequent development of addictions. A client example is discussed. Readers are invited to calculate their ACES score to facilitate awareness of the impact of trauma. A critique of attachment theory's bias toward white, middle class, heteronormative culture is included, as well as a subsequent study that includes a more diverse sample.

Early attachment relationships are explored through an overview of Dan Siegel's work in interpersonal neurobiology. This includes a detailed outline of the four styles of attachment and their relationship to autonomic states. A practice that explores early wounding and caregiver attachment styles is presented, helping you to link your early childhood experiences with subsequent trauma and addiction.

Deepening Your Trauma Story: Meeting Isabella (Practices 15–17)

It is common for the nervous system to shift into a dorsal dissociated state much of the time during childhood trauma. While this is protective, it also leads to large gaps in memory. As you move through the process of remembering and mourning bits and pieces of your trauma, history may start to come into consciousness. This can be alarming as murky fragments of memory surface. Remember three things. First, you are gaining skills in being with deep experiencing through Focusing and regulating your ANS. Second, whatever surfaces is in the past. While it can feel very real, it is not happening now. (This is assuming that you are safe enough now to be doing this work.) Third, you are not alone. You have a partner and/or therapist co-regulating with you.

As fragments come, pieces of your life start to integrate. Time and place begin to emerge into a cohesive narrative, bringing felt shifts. Over many months and years your understanding of how you came to be who you are creates a settled ventral felt sense. It is indeed a marvelous journey. It does require patience.

The next two practices help you deepen your trauma story. In preparation, I am going to share highlights of Isabella's journey.

MEETING ISABELLA, BUILDING A SAFE NEST

Rushing through my office door on a gloomy Friday morning, I hurry to open the blinds and put the kettle on. Overwhelming traffic has activated my nervous system and I take a moment to sit down and say hello to my inside quieter self. I remember to breathe and settle into a felt sense of ventral peace. Ahhhh, it feels so good to settle. I open my eyes to a brilliant splash of light as the sun breaks through a stormy sky. I allow myself to revel in these moments. They nourish the soul and bring healing energy into the wounded places that often emerge in this sacred space. Now I am ready for my first client of the day.

As I open the door to my waiting room I am struck by this young woman's presence. Isabella flashes me a smile as she swooshes by, making herself comfortable in the chair across from me. She looks around the room, taking her time to notice my big green leafy ferns, my coveted antique desk, painted a deep bold red, and my many, many books. Then she looks right at me with a big, warm gaze. Isabella wasn't afraid to connect with me right from the start. "I feel lost," she says. "I know that bad things happened to me when I was a little girl living in Italy, but I don't know what they are. No idea, I just know something bad happened. I have nightmares, and I can't eat sometimes." That was the beginning of our four-year relationship.

As time goes on, Isabella learns how to Focus and work with her nervous system, making her way around the 7 F states like a pro. She shares with me that she is an interior designer, and she likes the colors and shapes of the model. Isabella decorates her body in large, colorful fabrics that mirror her animated movements. Today, as she describes the sudden feelings of being lost, her head sways back and forth drawing attention to her long, elegant silver earrings. It seems that everything about this woman is in motion.

"I'm scared, Jan. I've been coming here for five months now, and at first, I felt better. I began to sleep better, to eat better, to work better. It felt so good to begin to calm myself down. Learning how to find my felt sense and regulate my nervous system was really helping me. But the last two weeks feel upsetting. I can't sleep, and I even binged on chocolate the other night which I hadn't done since we started working on the Four Circles. I don't get it. Why is this happening to me?" she asks, her cheeks flushing as her body surges into a sympathetic rush.

I know this place so well. Isabella is shifting into the second stage of healing, remembering and mourning. I talk with her about the healing process, reminding her that we have been working on establishing safety. She has done a wonderful job in learning how to be with her body, to welcome a quiet place inside. The safe nest container that we built is real. I invite her to feel into her grounded, ventral place. We pause and in she goes, feeling down into the felt sense of her grandmother's safe embrace. Her face relaxes, the little lines around her eyes melt away. Her jaw softens as she takes a sigh, deepening her level of experiencing to a 4 or 5 (Gendlin et al., 1969). We stay here for a while. Then she opens her eyes and says, "Thank you. Now I feel like me again. I don't know what happened to me."

"What happened to you is part of your healing journey. As you establish safety your body starts to settle, and more memories emerge. Memories that have been banished from awareness because your body dissociated them. Now that you feel safer, they are surfacing, wanting to be seen and heard and comforted. So, now we are ready to be with them. You have enough ventral energy to be with these lost parts. While we don't go digging them up, the ones that call to you need our help." Isabella nods, taking this all in.

"Often memories come in a disguised form. They appear as disturbing behaviors, like when you binge and purge, or in dreams and nightmares, or a shift into the trauma feedback loop for no apparent reason. Bodies talk to us in metaphors, so we have to listen with our Focusing ears."

Isabella nods, looking at me with a tired but relaxed gaze. Her eyes tell the story so poignantly. "That's enough for today," I say. "You have worked hard, now you need to rest your body. I recommend a warm bath with Epsom salts when you get home. Light some candles and let your body soak up the warm ventral energy of safety. Healing from trauma is a full-time job. It's exhausting."

ISABELLA'S RISKY RIDE: THE CONTEXT TELLS THE STORY

A few weeks later the phone rings and I reach for it as I am writing a few notes. "Jan, I'm so ashamed to tell you this. I'm at the police station."

"Isabella, is that you?" I ask, surprised, and not. This job is full of surprises.

"Yes," and there is a pause. I can hear her breathing heavily. I wait.

"I've been arrested for shoplifting."

I pause, taking this in. Years of being a trauma therapist have given me the wisdom to be with whatever comes, remembering that the context tells the story. Isabella's curious behavior will come to light with time.

"How can I help you, Isabella? Do you need a lawyer?"

"Not right now. They are letting me go, but I will have to get one."

"Do you want to come to see me? I have someone now but could see you this afternoon at two."

"Yes, I'll be there."

ISABELLA'S PARTS: THE HUNGRY ONE, THE LITTLE ONE, AND THE THIEF

We settle in with our Bengal spice tea. "Okay, Isabella, let's breathe." I make a point of meeting her gaze with all the warmth and love that I have grown to feel for her. Her nervous system needs to know that I am a safe person to explore all of this with. What an ordeal to go through. She starts by telling me what happened. This morning, she found herself in her favorite department store, the store she used to go to with her beloved grandmother when they both came to Canada.

She was standing at the counter, looking at the beautiful pink and gold swirls on the chocolate boxes. Tall sparkling blue boxes of caramels, yummy little yellow boxes of milk chocolates, and then her eyes find a bigger box of Swiss chocolates with almonds, her favorites, sitting just at the edge of the counter. She can't stop looking at these ones, thinking about the sweet smoothness as the chocolate glides down her throat. Sweet smoothness, sliding down into the anxious and gnarly place in her stomach, bringing the comfort of a warm numbing blanket. It's the only thing that helps.

As she says this, I see her begin to shift from a sympathetic flight state into the edges of dorsal. Her eyes glaze over as her hair falls across her face. I wait, keeping a close watch to make sure that she doesn't slip too far into a dorsal shutdown state. Then she looks up a bit, without eye contact but with enough presence, and starts to tell the story of how she stole the chocolates.

"I saw that box at the edge of the counter. I saw it, and I just wanted it, so I took it and put it in my bag. I don't remember what happened after that, not until I realized that a cop was asking me my name."

We pause and breathe. "You dissociated and lost some time there."

"Yes," she says, "I folded." Her eyes are beginning to glaze over.

"Are you with me now Isabella? Can you feel your feet on the floor?

"Yes, I'm just at the edges of dorsal," she says as she moves her feet. "I am moving my feet and pinching myself to stay with some ventral energy." We are both aware of how her body is shifting and blending states, learning how to regulate her nervous system so she can be with the trauma and not fall into it.

"What is happening in the center of your body?" We wait for a while, and then she says, "I feel churning in my stomach." Now I know that Isabella is connected to her body, deepening her level of experiencing. I move into step five in Focusing, asking into the memory part of the felt sense.

"Do you know this churning place? Is it familiar?"

We wait here for a minute. Then I see Isabella's body constrict as she struggles to make space for a painful memory to come.

In a whisper she says, "I am so ashamed. I used to steal things in this store." Tears pour down Isabella's anguished face.

"I am right here with you," I say softly. We are quiet for a while.

"After my mother beat me with the broom, I would go there and steal chocolates."

"Ah," I say. "That makes sense. The chocolate brought you comfort after the beating, and you had to steal to get it."

"Yaa!" she says, looking directly at me. Isabella experiences a powerful felt shift as she makes this significant connection. "I would steal money from her purse and buy chocolate, smooth, sweet, yummy, yummy little chocolates, or nutty chocolate bars, or sometimes chocolate ice cream. My little girl part, she's three years old," she says shyly. "She loves ice cream."

I see this little three-year-old appear in Isabella's body. "Hello Little One," I say gently, in a soft voice. She is an important part of the story, holding the wounds all by herself. Over time we want her to feel supported by Isabella's Inner Guide, her loving adult part.

Isabella pauses for a while, like she is lost in a fragmented memory. I wait, and then more comes. "The first time I remember mother beating me I was three. I hid in the closet and my grandmother, Nona, found me. She gave me chocolate ice cream." With that, Isabella's body collapses, falling back into the chair, looking for a place to hide.

NONA'S CHOCOLATE LOVE

Here we see Isabella's mind/body recovering a dissociated memory, beginning to make the connection between mother's abuse and grandmother's comforting chocolate.

Let's refer to our 7 F states to break this down. It's clear that Isabella has a disorganized attachment with her abusive mother. Her ANS has shifted into the trauma feedback loop to survive. Sugar, and specifically chocolate, has become associated with comfort after abuse, providing a hit of dopamine and forming an addictive trauma feedback loop. This behavior serves as a state regulation strategy to shift back and forth from a sympathetic to a dorsal state. Isabella's nervous system can't stay in dorsal forever, so her addictive behaviors help her to shift back to sympathetic so she can survive the horror.

There is a good chance that Isabella's grandmother acted out a dissociated trauma feedback loop of her own. Intergenerational trauma plays out in many ways. Perhaps when she was abused, she went to sugar for comfort, so she offers this to her granddaughter, giving Isabella the only help she knows how to give. What Nona doesn't realize is that because the sugar is coming from her, she has created a double reinforcement. *Nona's chocolate love is irresistible!*

ISABELLA'S CRITIC: THE VICE

I'm watching Isabella's body as she folds into the chair, tracking how far she fades into a dorsal state. "Are you in the closet?" I ask. "No," Isabella answers. "I'm under my bed. I used to hide there, to sleep at night."

"Is it okay to be there?" I ask. I'm titrating here, making sure that she isn't too close to the traumatic memory.

"Yes, I hear your voice, Jan, I am okay. Part of me is watching my little girl, my little one."

"Yes, we are here with her. She is not alone now. We are here to help her."

"She feels the vice."

"The vice?"

"Ya, the vice comes and attacks her saying horrible things. The vice says, *Get out of my sight. You make me sick.*"

"Who is the vice?" I ask. I am guessing that it's her mother, but I need to know if Isabella is aware of who it is.

"I don't know. It's a scary part that hurts the other parts. It sits in my throat, choking me like a vice. It's thick and slimy, and I can't talk. We must obey it."

Isabella suddenly jerks her head, looks up at me with sheer terror in her eyes and says, "We have to get out of here." I'm startled and pull back, then quickly settle. It's hard work to keep her safe.

With that sympathetic surge, I invite her (and myself) to feel her feet on the floor. "Now you can mobilize and get yourself out of there. You have an adult part that can help her get away to a safe place." Isabella is working hard to come back. "Listen to my voice," I tell her. "You are here now, with me, in my office. We are here together."

Isabella's body stands up, and I join her. We remain standing and I start into Practice 3 (The Pause), orienting her to the space around the room. She comes into her body and begins to sway back and forth, stamping her feet. "It feels good to move," she says. "I don't have to stay there!" She begins to settle, and we both sit down again, letting our bodies surrender to the support of the chair. We stay here, quietly resting for a while. You cannot rush this work.

"That was amazing," I say. "I love how your body knew to mobilize, to stand up and get out of there! A beautiful shift from dorsal to sympathetic to ventral states."

She smiles at me, standing and leaning in for a hug. We both arrive at a sweet spot of connection, a felt sense of deep coregulation. Picking up her gorgeous purple coat, she swooshes by me again. "See you next week!"

Yes, indeed. So much more to uncover as we integrate those vital connections from today's session. Next time we will work on the Trauma Egg. Isabella has recalled some essential fragments of her trauma story, and she can begin to develop a cohesive narrative. Now we are into the heart of it, remembering and mourning. We're making sense of horror, chaos, and the will to survive.

PAUSING

Let's pause here and reflect on Isabella's story. It's a striking example of how important it is to appreciate the context of your behavior. By listening compassionately to her embodied journey, we now understand how this very potent feedback loop of "Nona's chocolate love" was formed. No wonder her body developed an addiction to chocolate. It's all about survival.

Did you see yourself in Isabella's story? Did it activate any memories for you?

Notice how Isabella ended up compromising her own value system by stealing chocolate. How did this happen? Because she was acting out a learned habit, a trauma feedback loop that eased her unbearable pain. This behavior occurred in a dissociated state where her striatum (Motivational Engine) took over, diminishing access to her dorsolateral prefrontal cortex (Bridge of the Ship). Good people doing bad things.

Time for a break before you start into your Trauma Egg.

THE TRAUMA EGG

The Trauma Egg was created by Marilyn Murray (2012) over 30 years ago, and can be found online (https://www.shelleyklammer.com/post/trauma-egg -exercise). It is designed to help you document an inventory of traumatic life experiences. It can be overwhelming to complete it all at once, so you build it over time, as you move along in your healing journey. This helps you develop a linear timeline, connecting feelings to behaviors and events in your life. While it may be hard to face the significance of the trauma, the practice helps to face the truth about your life.

Making Your Trauma Egg

You will need a large piece of paper and lots of colored markers.

A. Draw a large egg shape on a piece of paper. Inside at the bottom of the egg, write "birth."
B. Above the egg, in the top left corner list Family Rules that you felt you were supposed to live by.
C. In the top right corner list Family Roles that you and others in your family adopted.
D. Below the egg, in the bottom left corner, list words that describe your father.
E. In the bottom right corner list words that describe your mother.

Inside the egg you draw separate little bubbles that represent traumatic experiences. Start at birth, the bottom of the egg, and add bubbles where you estimate them based on your age. Inside each bubble you put a drawing (no words), that symbolizes the experience. As you work through your trauma history felt sense experiences reveal themselves over time and are depicted inside each bubble. At first memories at different ages emerge, and with time you may find that more come to fill in empty spaces. As your egg develops you grow to understand how you became emotionally dysregulated and begin to construct a cohesive narrative of your life.

THE BACKGROUND FEELING

It is essential to remember that for some people, particularly marginalized groups, trauma is not one event, but rather a pervasive experience that colors all others. Gendlin called this the *background* part of the felt sense (1981, p. 90). He described it as the wallpaper on the walls of the inside space. It is always present, creating a quality or flavor to one's experiencing.

From a polyvagal lens, we can think of the background feeling as one's default neurophysiological state. Recall our discussion about how neurophysiological state determines our feelings and behavior. For example, if you live in a chronic state of flight/fight, the background feeling would be one of fear or anger. Background felt sense stories of intergenerational trauma, global trauma, such as world wars, or what we may see in the future with children who were born during the COVID-19 pandemic, may surface. Race, class, and gender oppression are part of this background felt sense. These experiences are vital in our understanding of trauma. Add a place for them to be written around the wall of the egg, symbolizing their all-encompassing presence, the wallpaper of our lived experiences.

*Practice 15. The Trauma Egg

Take time to settle into your familiar quiet space. Dropping down inside, invite a felt sense of grounding and safety to form and place a gentle hand where you feel it in your body. This will be your anchor as you travel back in time.

Bring to mind your image of the Trauma Egg, starting at birth and traveling along a timeline into childhood, adolescence, and adulthood. Ask yourself to find a time when you felt wounded. Notice what is happening, who is there, how old you are. Take time to be with all of this in your body, listening to what it needs.

When you are ready, you can open your eyes, and looking at your Trauma Egg decide where to place it: close to the bottom where you were born, or perhaps in the middle as you got older. Take time to reflect and share with your partner, noticing your felt sense of the journey as it is unfolding. Can you link life events to these experiences? Are there insights that come as you connect these events in your life? At first there may be many blank years that you don't remember. That is normal. Trauma fragments memory to protect us. But in order to understand your life, it is very helpful to link feelings and experiences with events.

Pause, and allow yourself to round this off inside. Feel your feet on the floor as you come back to the room, to your FSPM partner/therapist.

You will return to add to your Trauma Egg as you move through all the practices. Each time you can reflect, reprocess, and integrate new information. Sometimes major felt shifts occur, such as Isabella's memory of Nona's chocolate love. As she linked this to her stealing behavior, she had a moment of liberation from fear and shame. As she revisited this moment in her practices, she continued to rewire old shameful trauma feedback loops and build a strong ventral pathway.

A NOTE ABOUT MEMORY RETRIEVAL

Some of you will have very few narrative memories of events and time. It's common for people to have powerful body memories with little or no content. You may be able to connect with physical sensations, and perhaps an uncomfortable feeling, but with no additional information. This can be quite upsetting. It helps to remember that your body takes care of you by shutting down, dissociating much of what would be too alarming to process. But the truth comes in disguised forms. Your body tells the story in many ways. "Something happened," people say. "But was it real?" If you feel something in your body, try to greet it with respect and belief. Trust in your body's wisdom. Many people learn to live with lost parts, fragments of memories that may or may not reveal more with time. When you can validate them as real physical memories it helps to make peace with them. Often, with acceptance, they settle inside. It's important to know that you don't need to remember the whole story, just enough to help you make sense of your life.

FINDING AND WORKING WITH PARTS

Like Isabella, we all have different parts of ourselves. They tend to form with different experiences that happen to us and the subsequent roles we learned to play to help us survive. In our top-down culture we are taught that we are one person with one identity. But in the felt sense of life we know that we often hold two or more strong felt sense experiences about how we are experiencing any given moment. And each of these "parts" needs to be welcomed so that we can listen to the complexity within us. We are multidimensional beings. We can make space to engage with the murky edge of awareness.

As you build your Trauma Egg you will be experiencing different parts that emerge. Child parts that are tender and vulnerable, adolescent parts that are sometimes rebellious or sneaky, adult parts that reflect traumatic times through appeasing, collapsing, craving, demanding, and sometimes connecting/coregulating.

Some experiences are more potent than others and want more attention. They seem to be like separate parts of yourself that don't want to or can't form a cohesive whole "you." They may be dissociated like Isabella's little one, kept in a dorsal state, so unaware of other parts. Or stuck in Flight/Fight, full of fear or rage like her critic part, The Vice. They may be addicted parts that function in a trance state and hide, like the Thief who stole the chocolate.

The more that you can name the parts, noticing how they feel in your body, the more they can slowly feel connected to all the other parts. Working toward integrating all of your experiences and subsequent parts is a tough task. You need another, major player to step up and help. That part is your Inner Guide, the leader of the pack.

YOUR INNER GUIDE: BODY WISDOM

In addition to the many parts in your body, there is an "Inner Guide," a part that knows how to find a grounded ventral state of safety. In Lewis's terms it is the Bridge of the Ship, the part of you that is connected to your prefrontal cortex (Lewis, 2015). This part is good at planning, anticipating, organizing, and reflecting. It is insightful and compassionate, able to delay gratification. This part of you oversees all the other parts, guiding you in the direction of healing.

At times this bodily felt sense of connection may be faint, like a candle flickering in a hurricane. No matter how small, it is your anchor in the trauma storm. This part brought you to the healing journey, your body wisdom. Gendlin (1981) spoke of this part as an inner bodily felt sense of knowing. Just as your body knows how to heal a broken bone, it knows the right next step to heal from trauma, if, and this is vital, you give it what it needs.

*Practice 16. Working with Parts

Settle yourself in your private space. Invite your grounded self, your Inner Guide, to emerge. Slowly make your way down into the familiar space in the center of your body. By now you will have traveled down this body path many times. Take a moment to thank your body for all that has come before.

As you begin to explore the various parts, you can think of your safe, grounded, Inner Guide as a part of you that you already know. Even if it is small, it is important to be able to identify it and welcome it into the land of parts. You may want to spend some time with it before you begin to identify other parts of yourself. You can use one of your Body Cards to help you Focus.

When you are ready, invite the idea of different parts of you to come. One way to find a part is to think of a time when you felt torn by an inner conflict. One part of you wants one thing, and the other part wants another. Maybe one part of you wants to binge on chips, and the other part wants to be thin. One part wants to have lots of random sex, the other part wants to commit to a monogamous relationship. One part is appeasing, stuck in Favoring Others For Survival. The other part is rebelling in a Flight response. Notice all the parts that come, letting them begin to form.

Take time here to let a part, or parts, surface. Notice what comes. How old is this part? Does it have a name? A wish? A need? What drives it? What ANS state does it live in most of the time? Does it know your Inner Guide?

As you begin to round this off, take your time to come back to the room. Notice what state you are in. Ask your partner/therapist to coregulate with you, checking in to make sure that you are present. You can make a Process Recording and/or a Body Card for each part that emerges. With time you can build an array of Parts Body Cards that represent your inner world.

A NOTE ABOUT INTEGRATION

Integrating parts of you is key to healing. The more you can welcome all of you, the more you come alive.

Welcome Inner Diversity of Parts

As you heal, parts become acquainted with each other, easing the communication within. Like with any group, you do not all have to like each other all the time. But you do have to be able to create a safe enough inner landscape for all of the parts to feel okay. Having a strong, ventral Inner Guide is like having a secure attachment with a trusting parent. You become that parent to your own inner parts. You lead the way toward safety and respect, your North Star.

Learning to welcome the diversity of your parts helps in communicating with others. When you can speak about how a part of you feels something that may be vulnerable to share, it implies that not all of you feels this way. It lets the other person know that you can feel and think in different ways, indicating a flexibility and openness in your capacity to coregulate. For example, if a part of you is angry with someone, and another part of you empathizes with them, you can say, "A part of me is angry with you, and a part of me also understands why you did what you did." This creates a safer, more nuanced way of communicating that is often required in resolving conflicts. You are helping the other person's ANS to coregulate with you.

DISSOCIATIVE IDENTITY ADAPTATION

Some of you will find you have a growing awareness of many parts that do not communicate with each other. You may notice that you lose time and/or find yourself in places without remembering how you got there. Perhaps you receive emails or phone calls from people who claim to know you, but you do not know them. While this can be very scary, it is important to share with a therapist that you are experiencing this. You may have what is called, in the medical world, dissociative identity disorder. This means that you have many parts that are dissociated from each other.

From an embodied nonpathologizing lens we call this an adaptation, not a disorder. Again, the context tells the story. Your nervous system detected a high degree of threat, resulting in the need to dissociate parts so you could survive. Holding trauma in separate fragments created the capacity to stay alive. It just wasn't possible or wise to stay present in such a dangerous situation, so your ANS shut down. This is not an illness; it is a powerful example of the gift of dissociation. Think about it. *How else could you have survived such terrifying experiences?*

Now, with enough safety, it is possible to integrate these parts. It can be complicated, so it requires that you work with a therapist who is experienced in working with complex dissociation, preferably from an embodied, nonpathologizing perspective.

BORDERLINE PERSONALITY ADAPTATION

Perhaps you are someone who has been diagnosed as having borderline personality disorder. Put simply, this means that you have a part (or parts) that is rebellious, defensive, demanding, has violent mood swings, and often lacks empathy. These parts are very difficult to manage for you and for the people who are trying to help. Unfortunately, the current pathologizing psychiatric system doesn't understand them as biologically driven ways that the autonomic nervous system seeks survival.

From a polyvagal lens we understand these behaviors as part of a nervous system stuck in a trauma feedback loop, often fueled by a lot of fight energy. These difficult behaviors are the body's attempt to defend itself, to survive at all costs. Understanding the context in which these parts evolved tells the sad tale of why they evolved. Many people grew up with a parent stuck in a borderline pattern, swinging violently back and forth from sympathetic to dorsal, lacking the ability to empathize with family members. If you are raised in this trauma feedback loop, you continue to cycle back and forth, lost, and often abandoned by the system.

If this is you, you probably feel scorned, unlovable, misunderstood, and desperate. The tragedy here is that the trauma feedback loop is reinforced in the psychiatric system when "borderline behavior" is not understood through the lens of our autonomic nervous system.

Over 40 years ago, I had the fortune of being trained by Sandra Butler, one of the first people to write about incest (1978). She taught us that when a woman behaves in ways that are labeled borderline personality disorder, she is simply demonstrating what she learned to do to survive. I never forgot this. It became my mantra for understanding behavior.

Your borderline parts are welcomed in the Felt Sense Polyvagal Model. They are as lovable as any other parts of you. In fact, they need all the love they can get, for they have been handed a bad deck of cards. That can change now. You can learn to love your parts that are demanding, haughty, rageful, manipulative, or selfish when you understand that this is all they know how to do to stay alive. Together, with your FSPM partner/therapist, you can create enough safety for them to join the other parts. They are more than lovable, they are an essential part of you that deserves to be respected, given the hand you were dealt. As your Inner Guide encourages them to settle into safety they will seek connection with others. We are wired to connect, to socially engage and feel compassion for ourselves and others.

MANY MODELS FOR WORKING WITH PARTS

Recall that the Felt Sense Polyvagal Model provides a foundation upon which you may add many different theories. There are several ways of working with parts that have developed over time. The one that I learned was based on Multiple Personality Theory, reflected in Frank Putnam's work (1989). Bonnie Badenoch has developed a beautiful model called Inner Community Work (2011). Currently, Richard Schwartz's Internal Family Systems is a popular model (2019). Schwartz, Sweezy, and Sykes have recently published a book about Inner Family Systems and working with addiction (2023). Cece Sykes states the following in her earlier work with addiction:

> Viewed through an IFS lens, I see addiction as a chronic inner battle between two teams of protective parts: critical, controlling, and contemptuous managers, polarized with soothing, escapist, and distracting firefighters. Both sides are committed to preventing an overwhelm of underlying emotional pain (exiles). This includes use of substances, food, gambling, sex preoccupations, etc. (Sykes, 2016, p. 22)

Sykes's view of working with parts that are critical and parts that are distractors is compatible with the Felt Sense Polyvagal Model. Both IFS and FSPM are non-pathologizing models for treating trauma and addiction. They both address the pitfalls in engaging in power struggles with different parts of the self. We will explore this more as we work with the critic.

Janina Fisher has developed a model where she works with fragmented selves (2017). You may want to read about different ways of organizing your parts. Notice what language appeals to your felt sense of parts.

WORKING WITH THE CRITIC: CLEARING SPACE

The internal critic is a shaming part that often appears as a background feeling, with frequent bursts of attack. Many therapies focus a lot of attention on trying to tame the critic. It's understandable, as it can be such a powerful disruptor. It's very intimidating if it embodies the scary qualities of an abuser. It can also show up as a pervasive voice of doubt, constantly assessing and obsessing about your behavior, a quiet bully, wearing you down over time. By their very nature, critics invite a Fight/Flight response in our ANS.

Clearing Space, Step 1 in Focusing (see Chapter 3), is the basic skill that we use to manage critic attacks. The first task is to learn how to "clear the critic." To engage with the critic without having your Inner Guide in charge is dangerous. It simply reinforces the trauma feedback loop that you are stuck in. Many folks hear the critic voice when they are clearing space. You work with it as an issue that needs to be cleared along with all the others, getting the right amount of distance so that you can clear space. Or you may find that you are able to clear your issues, but there is a nagging sense of the critic that is a background feeling. Then you work with the background, asking it to clear.

You can use Clearing Space on its own, or as part of a full Focusing practice. It becomes a powerful skill that you draw on when you need to breathe and find some good ventral energy. As you practice clearing the critic you are building new neuropathways that strengthen each time you engage in distancing. Below find Clearing a Space from Practice 6 (Finding the Felt Sense: The 6 Steps of Focusing).

CLEARING A SPACE/CLEARING THE CRITIC: (STEP 1 IN FOCUSING)

Let your body guide you into sitting or standing in your private space. Gently soften your gaze and turn attention inwards. Say hello to whatever is there. Invite yourself to take a deep breath, following your awareness down somewhere into the center of your body. Ask yourself: "How am I today? What is coming between me and feeling okay?" Often four or five issues will be there in your life. One of them may be the critic. Name the issues one by one, without going into them, take each one at a time and imagine that you are putting it out in the hall, or even further away. You can come back to any one of these later. But for now, we want to make a clear space inside, to be able to breathe.

If one is particularly difficult, imagine floating it up into the air like a balloon, or you can put it in a boat and float it offshore. Let the issue know that you will return to it again. Just for now, we welcome a cleared space.

Eventually, with practice, the space down in the center of your body is clear. Notice what that is like. Find a handle for clearing the critic. Making a Body Card can serve as a resource when you are in the middle of a critic attack.

CLEARING SPACE BACKWARD

Sometimes you are so dysregulated in your body that asking the clearing space question, "Is there anything coming between me and feeling alright?" just doesn't seem appropriate. Too many things are getting in the way, and you are in a full-on sympathetic rush. Listing all the issues just makes it worse! Clearing space backward is a Focusing/mindfulness practice that encourages you to redirect attention to a space in your life, no matter how small, that brings relief.

Over time you are rewiring your brain, forming a new ventral feedback loop that associates a critic attack with the safety and resources of health, growth, and restoration. You can use this practice any time you feel overwhelmed in Fight/Flight/Fixate/Freeze/Fold.

*Practice 17. Clearing Space Backward

Settle yourself into your quiet, private space. Ask yourself the question, "Is there a place in my life, a moment in time, or a part of my body that feels okay?"

Often, the tip of your nose, or an earlobe, can feel clear. You bring attention to that place, practice staying with the sensations that arise. As you stay there you slowly invite the space to expand. When you find your mind wandering back to the voice of the critic, gently bring your attention back.

Allow yourself to rest in this space, noticing when you leave, and come back. Let your Inner Guide gently hold you in this space, allowing for lots of time to learn how to stay present in this quiet cleared space. Practice makes presence.

A NOTE TO PRACTITIONERS: DISARMING THE DISRUPTOR

We as clinicians need to inhabit a ventral state when we show up for our clients, especially when there is a bully in the room. It is helpful to imagine the fear that is fueling the critic. Often fear is at the heart of the critic's motivation to attack. So, we can think of the critic as a part that needs more safety in order to soften.

Modeling how to work with the critic can be very powerful for clients. Often, they are so traumatized by judgment that they are stuck in a Freeze or Fold response. When we show them how to manage the critic without fear, they learn how to coregulate with their Inner Guide who demonstrates ways of engaging, even befriending the critic, bringing it down to size.

You can disarm the critic by first grounding yourself in ventral and asking in a neutral and respectful tone "What are you so worried about?" Timing is everything when asking this question. When it works, and it often does, the critic will declare very clearly exactly what it is afraid of.

"The little crybaby needs to toughen up. She is always getting hurt, blabbing away to people, telling them too much, being too vulnerable. Then she makes dad angry, and he beats her. I have to try to protect her and clean up her mess."

Like the abusive parent, the critic has learned that it is unsafe to show vulnerability. Once we understand the critic's motivation, we can let them know we are all working toward the same goal, keeping the little girl and all the other parts safe. Protective critics are actually looking for guidance. After all, they are not mature parts. Once they trust that you are not afraid of them, they begin to align with you and eventually with your client's Inner Guide. You can form a powerful alliance that softens the relentless hold the critic has over the other parts.

Sometimes critics aren't willing to share their fear, they respond by telling you that they aren't worried about anything. Or they tell you in very impolite terms to buzz off! When this happens, you can simply try again when you think you may have a bit more of a connection with the critic. Or it may be that this critic is not going to engage. When this happens, it may be too dangerous to have the critic in the room. Then you must clear the critic. Establishing enough safety to heal is imperative. Either way, even when you are working with a critic that acknowledges fear, there are times when the voice of the critic will become activated under stress.

CHANGING THE FOCUS FROM CRITIC TO CRITICIZED

Another way of working with the critic was discussed by a seasoned Focusing-oriented therapist, Dieter Müller, a former psychology professor in Germany (2008). Müller suggested that we move from paying attention to the critic, to paying attention to the part that is being criticized, often the wounded child. Müller treats the critic as a "signpost" that connects us to the wounded parts who are waiting to be rescued.

Perhaps the critic has already taken up too much energy in the family of parts. Now it makes sense to identify and clear it, and then to focus attention on the damage that has been done, to strengthen these parts so that they will be able to heal. Remember, each time you visit a part with compassion, you are learning how to feel more whole, more present, more alive.

SUMMARY

Chapter 6 deepens the journey into remembering and mourning. It starts with a case example of Isabella uncovering the origins of her stealing behavior. We explore her different parts, including a child part, a critic, and a part she calls the Thief.

A detailed description of the Trauma Egg is included as well as a description of the background feeling that is often our default ANS state. Completing the Trauma Egg practice is followed by a practice in identifying different parts of the self and how they need to be welcomed. Reframing pathologized parts that are referred to as dissociative identity disorder and borderline personality disorder into dissociative identity adaptation and borderline personality adaptation brings a paradigm shift in understanding these states as attempts to survive.

Several ways of working with critic parts are discussed including Clearing Space, Clearing Space Backward, Disarming the Critic, and Using the Critic as a Signpost.

CHAPTER 7

Empowerment: Connection and Community (Practices 18–20)

We have arrived at the last chapter of this book, but by no means the end of your journey. Healing from trauma and addiction is often a lifelong experience. If you stay the course, life can become easier, more enjoyable, more meaningful. By now you know the course is not linear. You have no doubt circled back many times in your practices. It's a bit like climbing a mountain. You move along, slipping back at times, working hard, and resting. If you keep going, the climbing becomes easier, the resting more enjoyable. The more you climb and rest, the more your view expands. You see things very differently as you gain more distance. Your journey begins to make more sense. Now you realize there is no "top of the mountain." There is only the ongoing experience of your precious life.

Herman calls this last stage of healing reconnection (1992). Depending on the nature of your trauma, you may be reconnecting to a past life where having enough safety was a default state. For others with developmental trauma, establishing a sense of safety and connection is a completely new experience. Through your practices you have been laying the groundwork for this stage of healing. As you look up and out into the world there are endless possibilities for connection. You will be developing new empowering feedback loops infused with feelings of aliveness and intimacy.

THE EMPOWERMENT FEEDBACK LOOP

As your view of the world expands you begin to allow yourself to Flock, unfolding into social engagement with your community. Feeling safe enough allows you to take up more space, to build a felt sense of competence. The more you let yourself expand, the more you develop the confidence *to* expand. A new ventral feedback loop forms as your Inner Guide leads the way. Your autonomic nervous system feels safe enough to find home in Fun, Fired Up, Flock, and Flowing. Now you are experiencing the remarkable feeling of empowerment, the ability to be in charge of your own life. **Trauma robs us of our power. Healing reclaims our power as a natural state.** Trusting the process is easier when you remember how feedback loops work: What fires together, wires together. Your empowering behaviors are reinforced each time you allow yourself to expand.

Taking up space means stepping out into the world, seeking connection through community engagement. At first this can seem scary and overwhelming. We can break it down into steps. The first step is to feel into small moments of liberation. As you worked through your practices do you remember moments when you felt a shift from shaming and blaming into a sense of freedom? Recall our discussion about the polyvagal paradigm shift. The context tells the story. When Isabella understood why she stole the chocolate, it freed her from shame and blame. Likewise, when Patty understood how her abuse was shaping her life, she liberated herself from the shame and blame of overeating. Ian forgave himself for hiding in a dorsal state when he connected with the little boy part of him who had been so badly abused. These folks realized that they weren't sick or bad, their bodies were keeping them alive through engaging their ANS back up plan, the trauma feedback loop.

Practice 18 helps you explore the full felt sense of these moments of liberation through movement. When you invite your body to move with your feelings of expansion, you deepen and reinforce the felt sense. Some of you will find this a natural way to access moments of liberation. For others, you will want to take it slowly at first. It may feel overwhelming as you allow yourself to expand out into space. Feeling self-conscious is normal, so you may want to practice on your own in the beginning. Playing some of your favorite music can help you relax into movement. Does your body enjoy jazz, rhythm and blues, classical music, or hard rock? India Arie's song "I Am Light" is a beautiful accompaniment to this practice.

You can practice with your FSPM partner. Of course, you can also experience moments of liberation on the dance floor. This is coregulation in action!

*Practice 18. I Am Light: Moments of Liberation

Find a large space to do this practice. It may be in a park or in your basement. Notice what your body needs as you prepare. Slowly drop your awareness down into the center of your body. Allow yourself to feel into a moment along your journey where you experienced a felt shift in your body, a physical expansion of release, and a sense of recognizing your body's wisdom in helping you heal. You realize that your problem behaviors, whether they are addictive or dissociative, or both, have helped you survive. Now you are ready to let them go, bit by bit. You are beginning to move out into the world with clarity and presence.

As you find the felt sense of your liberating moment, gently invite your body to move, allowing your arms and legs to open to the space around you. Breathe and welcome all of you into the room. Take up as much space as you feel safe to explore. Say to yourself, "I am liberating myself from shame and blame." Let yourself feel the power to move, to stretch out, to breathe into the space around you, without confinement. Move, stretch, breathe, expand . . . move, stretch, breathe, expand . . .

FINDING YOUR WHOLE SENSE OF SELF

As your body unfolds, your Inner Guide, your sense of self, expands. Stretching into space allows you to take charge of your body and your life. This feeling of empowerment gives you the courage and desire to define who you are, to recognize that you can shift out of Fighting and Folding and Favoring Others for Survival. In a recent conversation with Dr. Ruth Lanius, a world-renowned trauma clinician and researcher, we explored the vital importance of finding your whole sense of self:

"We think about concentration difficulties, flashbacks, nightmares, avoidance, numbing. Too much arousal. Too little arousal. Shame, guilt, anger, terror, fear. But I think what it all boils down to is that a lot of traumatized individuals actually lose the sense of who they are after trauma. Or if we're dealing with developmental trauma, they actually never form a coherent whole sense of self" (Lanius, 2024).

DEFAULT MODE NETWORK

Dr. Lanius goes on to describe how this sense of self is understood in terms of brain development (2023). The default mode network is a brain network that is connected when individuals are at rest—not focused on a task, just connecting to an inside state of interoception. It engages when we are reflecting on what we are feeling and as we are remembering events. It helps us to read the emotions, intentions, and feelings of others. The social engagement system is part of the default mode network. We feel connected to others in a restful, safe context.

In the aftermath of trauma the default mode network becomes very disconnected. Generally speaking, the back part of the network helps us remember the past, and the front part of the network gives the past a context. It gives you the context for what is happening now, so you can distinguish between the present and what you are recalling from a past event. But as you probably know so well, triggered memories from past trauma feel like they are happening now. That's because the default mode network becomes very disconnected, and only the back part of this network is active. You become stuck in the past, without awareness of the present context.

The only time this network seems to become somewhat connected is under threat. So, when people are faced with reminders of their trauma, when they get that intense hyperarousal, that's the only time we see this network come online. So that's the only time we see that they have this semblance of a sense of self. When we first saw this, we were really struck by these findings. I invited a trauma survivor to get her sense of what she felt as she looked at these data, and she described eloquently how she engaged in regular stealing. When she stole, she would get that intense hyperarousal, and that was the only time she felt alive. Her sense of self would come online (Lanius, 2023).

This is a profound finding. It makes sense when you think about living in the trauma feedback loop. The only way to feel alive and connected to others is when you shift out of the deadened state of the dorsal vagus and into the sympathetic surge of heightened aliveness. If that sense of aliveness and connection is only present when you feel threatened, this may be what keeps you in an unsafe, abusive relationship. It would also explain why some of you may be stuck in a rageful spiral, hurting yourself and those around you. Porges often reminds us that being socially connected is a biological imperative (2023). Your brain/body is doing what it needs to do to survive, to stay connected to others, even when it hurts. Remember, you don't consciously choose to shift into the trauma feedback loop. Neuroception is happening at a subconscious level where the primitive part of your brain is online.

Let's pause here and reflect. When do you feel most alive? Is your sense of "you" most present when you are in Flight/Fight? Is this changing as you heal?

As you move through the practices you are beginning to develop your Inner Guide, a sense of yourself that is based on firmer ground. In a Flock state, you shift how you define yourself. When your felt sense of safety prevails, you begin to experience life in a different way. You can think more clearly as your prefrontal cortex comes online. You can plan, pace, and pause. You feel like a different person, or a different part of you is developing. With your new understanding you realize that you are not masochistic, or untreatable, or weak and hopelessly addicted. Your brain has been driving this behavior to keep you alive. And now, with this awareness you can change your behavior through your FSPM practices.

AUTHENTICITY VERSUS ATTACHMENT

So, who is the authentic you? That is the big question. After all that you have been through, there is a "you" in there that is emerging. A "you" that is longing for safety and social connection. A "you" that needs to feel safe to be authentic.

In Gabor Maté's book, *The Myth of Normal* (2022), he explores this connection between safety, authenticity, and our attachment history. He defines authenticity as "knowing our gut feelings when they arise and honoring them" (Maté, 2022, p. 106). The practices in this book are teaching you how to connect with your gut feelings through exploring your felt sense. This is the source of your authentic self, your embodied Inner Guide.

Once you have a felt sense of your gut feelings, the next step Maté suggests is developing the capacity to honor them (2022). It's one thing to know what feels right. It's quite another thing to be able to honor it, to act on it. This is especially challenging when it goes against the wishes of others. Then you are faced with a threat of loss or disapproval in your attachment with others.

Maté calls this the "traumatic tension" between our need for authenticity and our need for attachment (2022). These needs are deeply rooted in our biology. We know our need for connection is a biological imperative. Without a secure attachment, we threaten our survival. This tension is particularly relevant in two of the attachment styles, Fawning and Favoring Others for Survival, that we explored in Practice 5 (The Felt Sense of Neuroception).

If your ANS was shaped by a trauma feedback loop that included these states, you have a heightened sense of protecting yourself by pleasing, placating, and serving others. In unsafe environments disagreeing, arguing, or saying no can be life threatening. While these behaviors hurt you, they also helped you. Those of you in marginalized groups will resonate with these states. They are default for survival.

As you begin to heal, and your sense of self evolves, you will be challenged to address the tension between your own integrity and what others ask of you. Some of you have traveled this terrain, making the very hard and painful decision to distance from destructive relationships with family, partners, and friends. While these courageous acts are scary, the more you build a safe nest, the more you feel empowered to explore, to grow, to become all that you are. Remember, without enough safety you cannot heal. This means that addressing relationships where you are sacrificing your authenticity for attachment is a necessary part of healing. This is one of the most challenging aspects of your journey. You will need a lot of coregulation to be able to face this part of your path. Your FSPM partner and your compassionate community become an essential support.

Trauma constricts us, authenticity expands us. Your daily practices will keep you aware of neuroception and interoception, your basic skills for finding safety and connection.

COMMUNITIES OF COMPASSION: FLOCKING AND UNFOLDING

To sustain a state of health, growth, and restoration human beings need to connect in communities of compassion. The more you reach out to connect with others, the more your body will thank you for the rich sustenance. Sustained connection with larger community engagement helps us to feel a sense of belonging and find meaning and direction. Many trauma survivors reap huge rewards in joining social movements of liberation. Trauma shatters meaning, but out of the rubble new meaning emerges.

As the understanding of trauma develops, communities are sprouting up around you. How do you know what communities are safe enough to explore? How do you keep yourself safe as you take up more space and become more adventurous in the world? Remember the power of coregulation. You and your FSPM partner can explore together. You can compare notes and your felt sense of different communities that you visit, online, or in-person.

It is helpful to become familiar with different kinds of communities. You can spend some time with your partner exploring your interests and ideas. Notice how each community organizes itself. Who is the leader? What is their purpose? Do they address issues of safety and trust? What are the rules of engagement in their online presence and in-person gatherings? Notice if they honor body wisdom. Do they address marginalized groups? Most of all, what is your felt sense of the group? Do you feel authentic when you are in the community? Is this your tribe? Below are some communities that are connected with the Felt Sense Polyvagal Model.

Polyvagal Institute (polyvagal.org)

Randall Redfield, cofounder and executive director of the Polyvagal Institute, offers the following description:

> When I'm asked to describe the institute, invariably one of my favorite sayings of Dr. Porges comes to mind: "social connection is a biological imperative." The Polyvagal Institute's role is to enhance social connectivity by making Polyvagal Theory more accessible through education and community. Helping others understand how the feelings of safety and threat underlie our behavior and health provides a huge service. The joy of this work, to me, is in seeing how individuals change and communities develop when people discover the transformative power of addressing our fundamental need for safety. We know from Polyvagal Theory that when individuals feel safe, they respond with compassion. In an age that's plagued by a profound sense of isolation and the need to connect, our mission is more important than ever. (Redfield, personal communication, 2024)

The Polyvagal Institute (www.polyvagalinstitute.org) is the home of the Felt Sense Polyvagal Community. Within the institute, there are courses available to the general public. Several of these courses are given by Dr. Porges and Deb Dana, a clinical social worker and leading trauma therapist. Dana has brilliantly translated this complex theory into language that makes it accessible to those of us not trained in neuroscience. This has had a huge impact on our field of trauma and addiction.

For those of you interested in professional training I offer a training program through the Polyvagal Institute (https://www.polyvagalinstitute.org/items/felt-sense-polyvagal-model:-a-certificate-for-treating-trauma-and-addiction) that equips you to become a Felt Sense Polyvagal Facilitator. The Polyvagal Institute has an app that allows you to connect with several different kinds of interest groups. With our Felt Sense Polyvagal Model community I interview trauma and addiction experts on a free live Zoom series called Embodied Dialogues once a month (https://www.youtube.com/c/JanWinhall). We also connect with each other in an online chat and meet at live international events.

Felt Sense Polyvagal Trauma/Addiction Groups (janwinhall.com)

Online Felt Sense Polyvagal Trauma/Addiction Groups are offered by trained FSPM Facilitators who have completed the three-course training on the polyvagal institute website. Leaders use this book to guide people through the 20 practices. Each person is matched with a FSPM partner at the beginning of the journey. Often these partnerships become lifelong lifelines. You can find information about these groups at janwinhall.com.

International Focusing Institute (focusing.org)

Mary Hendricks-Gendlin, PhD, former director of The Focusing Institute describes the power of Focusing: "Focusing is a force for peace because it frees people from being manipulated by external authority, cultural roles, ideologies, and the internal oppression of self-attacking and shame. This freeing has to do with an ability to pause the ongoing situation and create a space in which a felt sense can form" (2003).

The International Focusing Institute is a second home for the Felt Sense Polyvagal Community. The Institute is an international, cross-cultural organization dedicated to supporting people worldwide who practice, teach, and develop

Focusing and its underlying philosophy. It also promotes Focusing research and is an information hub for Focusing-related literature and trainings to become a Focusing Trainer or Focusing Oriented Therapist. The Focusing community hosts international conferences regularly that are intellectually stimulating and deeply embodied. The Institute is committed to sharing and advancing the work of its founder, Eugene Gendlin, and those who have built on his legacy. You can find a Focusing partner through their website at focusing.org.

Focusing Initiatives International (focusinginternational.org)

Focusing Initiatives International is another Focusing community that promotes social change by supporting people and communities to develop wellness, inner healing, and creative solutions to local problems. It is based on a belief that human beings thrive when they are physically and emotionally safe, and also free to secure their needs and shape their communities in ways that hold meaning for them.

Focusing Initiatives International provides consultation, collaborative program development, and support for community efforts to apply the methods and wisdom of Focusing practices to the specific needs of their local situation. They work with marginalized populations and/or people who have few resources to cover the costs of services that are often lifesaving. Much of their work is with minoritized populations and people recovering from disasters or wars.

Polyvagal Informed Yoga Community (drarielleschwartz.com)

For those of you who are yoga practitioners, or are curious about exploring yoga, Arielle Schwartz has developed a warm and embracing community of online and in-person events. Arielle's knowledge of Polyvagal Theory and other healing modalities is impressive. Combining a yoga practice with your FSPM Daily Practices helps to enhance your healing.

> Compassion is the key that releases us from our own pain, and it helps us serve others.
>
> We move beyond our self-consciousness or fear of inadequacy. With this freedom, we are more likely to offer the gift of our presence to others. Perhaps we feel inspired by a sense of purpose or a longing to be of greater service to this world. (Schwartz, 2024, p. 176)

Embodied Ancestral Inquiry (wildbody.ca)

Embodied Ancestral Inquiry (EAI) is a methodology for understanding and working with intergenerational trauma and white supremacy through somatic practice
and research. As we listen for the stories our bodies tell about how we came to be
where we are, we can begin to heal the legacies of supremacy held in our bodies,
and create room for more possibility, choice, and action toward repair. We all come
from people who at one time had deep and reciprocal relationships to the land,
healing and spiritual practices, and a rooted sense of belonging. Tracing our ances-
try in embodied ways offers us an opportunity to feel into how our people became
severed from these ways of life and learned to inflict supremacy and domination
onto others. We can transform these cycles of harm and leave a different path forward for our descendants. (Heinrichs, personal communication, 2024)

In Practice 13, The Wheel of Privilege, you explored your social identity. One
aspect that arose for some of you is the way in which you can be part of a privileged group that has harmed others. How does that impact how you see yourself?
Do you carry shame about this, and/or feel threatened and defensive? How can
you transform this pattern? Marika Heinrichs's EAI community explores a path
toward liberation for all peoples. Informed by Focusing, generative somatics,
critical race theory, postcolonial history, and Polyvagal Theory, it is highly political and deeply somatic.

Polyvagal Play Zone (polyvagalinstitute.org/items/the-play-zone:-a-neurophysiological-approach-to-our-highest-performance)

Michael Allison is an advocate for the value of play in the embodied healing
of trauma:

Interactive, reciprocal, and spontaneous play provides us with an opportunity
to enhance our capacity to navigate a variety of physiological states which builds
resilience and flexibility within the nervous system. As we communicate with
one another in play through voice, facial expression, body language, and listening,
we functionally recruit the neural mechanisms that integrate directly with the
vagal regulation of our heart, lungs, and internal environment. Instead of getting

locked into any one bodily state, play enhances vagal efficiency, our ability to rapidly move between states and access the social engagement system in the face of challenge. (Allison, personal communication, 2024)

Michael Allison has created a polyvagal community through the Polyvagal Institute that focuses on bringing together awareness of autonomic state and the role of play to help individuals move into ventral states that support the experience of joy, curiosity, surprise, connection, and celebration. If your nervous system is stuck in a mobilized state of defense, play can offer an opportunity to connect with others in a safe activity, inviting your body to relax, open, and expand. Play also gets the body moving and gently invites connection when you feel overwhelmed, withdrawn, and hiding in dorsal.

Mobilizing through movement provides a pathway toward believing that it is safe to trust again. Maybe it's time to take dancing lessons, sing in a choir, join a team sport, or start playing music in a band. Allison reminds us that through safe playful interaction with others, you can feel a powerful sense of connection, camaraderie, and collaboration that you could never achieve on your own. Michael gives us a beautiful example of playful coregulation.

It occurred in the 1984 production of "We Are the World," as seen in the 2024 Netflix documentary *The Greatest Night in Pop*. In a gathering of more than forty of the greatest pop stars at that time, Bob Dylan, who was considered an icon, was so overwhelmed with having to perform to the expectations placed upon him, while simultaneously being surrounded by so many amazing singers, he literally couldn't find his voice. At one point, he was not only unable to sing, but he struggled to make any kind of sound resonate from his body, as he began to fall into a state of collapse.

Quincy Jones recognized what was happening, and quickly came alongside Bob. With a soft, gentle, and supportive tone of voice, as if talking to a child, Quincy lifted Bob just enough such that Bob then reached for more support through his friend Stevie Wonder. With the two of them at the piano, Stevie ventriloquized Bob's voice as they sang and played together. This spontaneous, reciprocal, and playful interaction reassured Bob's paralyzing anxiety with safety and connection, and reassured Bob's body that it was actually safe enough to sing, to play, and to share his voice with the world. In the end, Bob "sang his heart out," and everyone celebrated his solo performance and what they all were able to do together through play! (Allison, personal communication, 2024).

These are just a few of the many communities of compassion that are available to explore. As you look ahead, finding other interest groups or faith-based groups can be an excellent way to expand your worldview and your sense of self. Allow yourself to play with ideas of how you can expand: cooking, gardening, pickle ball. There's a big, wide world of opportunities.

REFLECT, DIGEST, MAKE A PLAN

As this book comes to an end, it's important to pause and take time to reflect, digest, and then plan ahead on your continued cycle of climbing and resting. In preparation for Practice 19 you will need to gather the FSPM model of 7 F states, your book, your Four Circles, all of your journals, Process Recordings, Body Cards, and anything else that you use as a resource. Find a large surface to work on.

You will do this practice in two steps so you can slowly take in the whole of it. Over time you will do many rounds, returning to it as you plan ahead. Reflecting and digesting gives you time to develop new pathways of integration.

An important note: remember pacing as one of your 5 P's. You may not be ready to take in your timeline as a whole. If so, just take in little parts of your journey at a time, carefully titrating your experience. As you proceed you will be able to integrate all your practices. Your Focusing partner/therapist can help you with this.

Practice 19. Your Embodied Timeline: Review and Reflect

Step One

Bring yourself into your private space, settling and inviting some good energy into your body. You have worked so hard, now it is time to reflect on where you were and where you are now. **With your eyes open,** *lay out your Body Cards and Process Recordings in chronological order. The first time you do this just* **lightly touch each practice,** *looking at your Process Recordings and Body Cards. You want to get a sense of the whole of it as it expands over time.*

Now that you have taken in your whole journey, **close your eyes** *and bring your attention inside. Let your body begin to form a felt sense of the path. Now you have an embodied timeline of your healing journey.*

Make a Body Card and Process Recording of your embodied timeline.

Step Two

As you lay out your timeline again, notice how it feels to be with all of it. Let yourself go through each practice in chronological order, remembering how you felt when you began and what you have learned along the way. You are embodying a cohesive narrative of your whole life history. This may be the first time that your brain/body is consciously integrating the pieces, weaving together lost moments that drifted on their own. Now you are anchoring them in your body history. As you do this you are healing your default mode network. Past connects with present, and body connects with brain.

Invite a felt sense to form.

Make a Body Card and Process Recording.

MORE ROUNDS OF THE EMBODIED TIMELINE

As you continue this practice with more rounds, slow the process down and invite your body to show you where it wants to linger along the timeline. What wants your attention now? You want to go there and explore how it feels to be in and with your body now. As you heal you will find more information emerging. Is there more to add to your Trauma Egg as your memories surface? Do you want to work on developing your Four Circle practice? Over months and years, you will return to your timeline, exploring, digesting, spending time where your felt sense is drawn.

Sharing with your partner powerful insights that have formed through each part of the journey will be very helpful. Reflecting activates the process of integration. With each review you integrate more and more of your life story, shifting into the empowerment feedback loop. Your experiences are understood in a new trauma informed context with powerful felt shifts along the way.

DAILY/WEEKLY HEALING PRACTICES

Now that you have completed the first round of practices you will need to continue your daily check-ins on your own as a baseline. They are an essential part of maintaining your self care. Checking your 7 F states and your Four Circles as you begin your day provides you with an embodied roadmap.

You will need to meet with your FSPM partner/practitioner and decide on your next steps. Will you continue to partner? If not, you will need to look for a new partner, group, or community with the links provided or through your own research. You may find that meeting once a week with your partner is a good fit for you.

Pacing is important. If you are actively trying to reduce harm with bad habits, and/or you are feeling extreme ANS dysregulation, you will need to meet daily. You can negotiate a 20-minute check-in and then a longer Focusing session once or twice a week.

You can also have a conversation about how you might use text messaging. You can arrange to text if you feel overwhelmed, without the expectation of your accountability partner/therapist will respond unless you ask for an emergency meeting. This provides 24-hour support for you, and it is not as onerous for partners/therapists. Healing from trauma and addiction requires around the clock support at different times along the way. This is normal and needs to be provided to maximize healing outcomes. **An ideal model to use is to have both an FSPM accountability partner who attends your FSPM group as well as a therapist.**

CELEBRATING YOU: A MIXED BAG

In this final chapter we have been focusing on feeling good, happy, empowered, even joyous and intimate with others. But what if all of this feels too overwhelming and dangerous?

This is a normal response. It shows that you are probably in stage two, remembering and mourning, and not ready to venture out of your safe enough nest yet. Keep going, climbing, and resting, and at some point, you will feel a shift, a readiness to peek out at the world. Your head will lift up more, you will look more people in the eye and have short bursts of happiness. Moments that used to feel intensely uncomfortable, like you want to get away from yourself, will be soothed by your Inner Guide.

You cannot force this shift in states. You can keep coming back to befriending your body, befriending your community, step-by-step. One day you will find yourself with a warm group of friends, celebrating a moment of safety and connection. **You realize that what you have lost in innocence, you have gained in wisdom.** While it is a hard-won journey, despite all your suffering, joy refuses to die.

*Practice 20. A Celebration Practice in Three Steps

Practice 20 celebrates you and your journey with your partner. You can do this practice three ways: in your quiet private space, in a large space moving to music, and together in coregulation with your partner.

1. FLOWING, FLOCK, FUN, FIRED UP: Dropping Down Inside

Come into your quiet, private space, appreciating how this safe container has supported you. As you close your eyes, bring your attention down into this familiar place in the center of your body. Finding your Inner Guide, invite a felt sense of deep appreciation for yourself in completing this first round of the FSPM journey. Notice what comes, as you allow yourself to invite a celebration of you. How does your body carry feelings of pride, accomplishment, confidence, and compassion for yourself? Let your body travel through Flowing, Flock, Fired Up, and Fun, noticing the felt sense of empowerment as you appreciate the newer expanding sense of you. Find a handle for this place of celebration.

Make a Body Card and/or Process Recording to mark this moment.

2. FUN, FIRED UP: Moving to Music

Find a large space to spread out. Listening to music (such as the wonderful song "Celebration" by Kool and the Gang) will mobilize your sympathetic nervous system. Standing in your space, take some time to find your felt sense of celebrating you. Once you hear the beat follow your body into Fun and Fired/up, gliding into the large space around you. Your body will thank you for creating a playful, safe space to honor your accomplishments.

Make a Body Card and/or Process Recording to mark this moment.

3. FLOCKING: Celebrating Your Partnership in Coregulation

Together with your partner take some time to drop down inside and invite a felt sense of your Focusing partnership. Notice the qualities of your partner that have helped you to heal, how you have coregulated along the way, how your body appreciates your partner's healing journey. You have both traveled into messy, scary, and marvelous terrain together in a safe-enough container. Welcome and celebrate your intimate journey!

Find a handle for celebrating your relationship. Invite your partner to do step two with you, moving together in an empowering dance of deep embodied appreciation for each other. Move, stretch, breathe, expand . . .

Make a Body Card and/or Process Recording to mark this moment.

You and your partner have arrived in this moment of completion, yet also know that the path is a circle. You will arrive here again and again, as practice makes presence.

The world is in turmoil. It is a very challenging time for everyone. It is my hope that you will find moment by moment safety as you venture out into unfamiliar places, knowing that you can return to your well-worn path of 20 embodied practices. Having a safe-enough nest to come home to makes for well-deserved moments of empowerment. You have both shown great courage and endurance. Now it's time to rest and enjoy!

SUMMARY

Chapter 7 introduces the third and last stage of Herman's healing journey, reconnection (Herman, 1992). If you experienced developmental trauma your journey will be one of connection with the world for the first time in a new, fresh way, that is grounded in enough safety. The empowerment feedback loop is discussed as the ventral pathway of coregulation.

Practice 18 invites you to celebrate moments of liberation from shame and blame. You shift into understanding your troubling behaviors as adaptive responses that helped you to survive. You learn to move, stretch, breathe, and expand into a sense of freedom.

Ruth Lanius's (2020) work in identifying the default model network illuminates the importance of understanding how the brain is damaged because of trauma, leading to a disruption in a sense of self and time. An exploration of the authentic self is discussed through Gabor Maté's concept of authenticity versus attachment (2022).

There is a strong emphasis placed on the importance of finding a compassionate community to support your healing journey. Several examples are given including the Felt Sense Polyvagal Community online trauma and addiction groups.

Practice 19, Your Embodied Timeline, brings together your healing journey into one cohesive narrative. Direction is given on how to proceed with your healing path. The book closes with Practice 20, describing ways to celebrate you and your partner.

Conclusion

The Felt Sense Polyvagal Model (FSPM) is a radical departure from the norm. Traditional models of talk therapy try to figure problems out in your head, using your thoughts as your guiding light. This is a tragic mistake.

Our culture has forgotten that we live in our bodies. But our bodies have not forgotten us. As you know by now, the body speaks to us in many ways. The FSPM has taught you how to listen to your body's language, to neuroception and interoception. In so doing, you begin the marvelous paradigm shift, transforming your touchstone for healing from your head, down into your whole body, from head to toe, and toe to head. This bidirectional pathway, illuminated by your 20 embodied practices, connects you with the vagus nerve and the felt sense. This becomes your Inner Guide. This changes everything.

While Western culture favors top-down left hemisphere thinking, as you descend into the body you shift paradigms into bottom-up right hemisphere experiencing. A sense of aliveness emerges as you come into your center, breathing into connection with yourself, other people, and all living creatures. As you work on your embodied timeline you slowly weave together past with present, using your left hemisphere to construct the linear timeline and your right hemisphere to find the felt sense of your experience. Continuing your journey of integration, you and your partner climb and rest, moving upwards, taking in the whole vista, the felt sense of your life.

In embracing the Felt Sense Polyvagal Model you join with others in becoming part of a new social movement of embodied liberation. Liberation from shame and blame. While it may seem small, it is a fiercely loving and rapidly increasing community of people. People who are passionate about changing the face of treatment for healing from trauma and addiction. Embrace community, stay the course.

Appendix: Organization Links

Name	Link
Polyvagal Institute	polyvagal.org
Jan Winhall	1. janwinhall.com 2. https://www.polyvagalinstitute.org/items/felt-sense-polyvagal-model:-a-certificate-or-treating-trauma-and-addiction 3. https://www.youtube.com/c/JanWinhall
International Focusing Institute	focusing.org
Focusing Initiatives International	focusinginternational.org
Arielle Schwartz	drarielleschwartz.com
Embodied Ancestral Inquiry	wildbody.ca
Michael Allison	polyvagalinstitute.org/items/the-play-zone:-a-neurophysiological-approach-to-our-highest-performance

References

Ainsworth, M. D. S. (1967). *Infancy in Uganda: Infant care and the growth of love.* Baltimore, MD: The Johns Hopkins University Press.

Ainsworth, M. D. S., Blehar, M. C., Waters, E., & Wall, S. (2015*). Patterns of attachment: psychological study of the Strange Situation.* New York: Routledge.

Alexander, B. (2008). *The globalization of addiction: A study in poverty of the spirit.* Oxford University Press.

Bass, E., & Davis, L. (1988). *The courage to heal: A guide for women survivors of child sexual abuse.* Perennial Library, Harper & Row.

Badenoch, B. (2008). *Being a brain-wise therapist: A practical guide to interpersonal neurobiology.* Norton.

Bowlby, J. (1969). *Attachment and loss, Vol. 1: Attachment.* Basic Books.

Butler, S. (1978). *The conspiracy of silence: The trauma of incest.* Volcano Press.

Carnes, P. (2001). *Out of the shadows: Understanding sexual addiction.* Hazelden.

Dawson, N. (2018). From Uganda to Baltimore to Alexandra Township: How far can Ainsworth's theory stretch? *South African Journal of Psychiatry, 24*, 1137. doi.org/10.4102/sajpsychiatry.v24i0.1137

Doidge, N. (2007). *The brain that changes itself: Stories of personal triumph from the frontiers of brain science.* Viking.

Doidge, N. (2017). *The brain's way of healing.* Penguin Books.

Felitti, V. J., Anda, R. F., Nordenberg, D., Williamson, D. F., Spitz, A. M., Edwards, V., Koss, M. P., & Marks, J. S. (1998). The relationship of adult health status to childhood abuse and household dysfunction. *American Journal of Preventative Medicine. 14*, 245–258.

Felitti, V. J. (2002). The relation between adverse childhood experiences and adult health: Turning gold into lead. *Permanente Journal, 6*(1), 44–47.

Felitti, V. J. (2004). The origins of addiction: Evidence from the adverse childhood experiences study. English version of the article published in Germany as; Felitti V. J. Ursprunge des Suchtverhaltens – Evidenzen aus einer Studie zu belastenden Kindheitserfahrungen. Praxis der Kinderpsychologie und Kinderpsychiatrie, *52*, 547–559.

Felitti, V. J. (2016). *Addiction, trauma and adverse childhood experiences* (ACES's): *The neuroscience behind developmental attachment, trauma, and adverse childhood experiences.* Eau Claire, WI: PESI.

Felitti, V. J. (2019, February 7). How childhood can haunt us. *Podcast.* Retrieved from https://www.acwsconecction.com/blog/how-childhood-can-haunt-us -mowe-blog-podcast.

Fisher, J. (2017). *Healing the fragmented selves of trauma survivors: Overcoming internal self-alienation* (1st ed). Routledge.

Frankl, V. E. (1984). [Quote]. Retrieved from https://www.psychologytoday.com/ca/blog/hide-and-seek/201205/mans-search-meaning.

Gendlin, E. T. (1964). A theory of personality change. In P. Worchel & D. Byrne (eds.), *Personality change*, pp. 100–48. John Wiley & Sons.

Gendlin, E. T. (1990). The small steps of the therapy process: How they come and how to help them come. In G. Lietaer, J. Rombauts & R. Van Balen (Eds.), *Client-centered and experiential psychotherapy in the nineties*, pp. 205–224. Leuven: Leuven University Press.

Gendlin, E. T. (1996). *Focusing oriented psychotherapy.* Guilford Press.

Gendlin, E. T. (1978/1981). *Focusing.* Bantam.

Hebb, D. O. (1949), *The organization of behavior: A neuropsychological theory.* Wiley & Sons.

Hendricks-Gendlin, M. (2003). *Focusing as a force for peace: The revolutionary pause.* [Conference]. Fifteenth Focusing International Conference, Germany. https://focusing.org/social-issues/hendricks-peace

Herman, J. (1992). *Trauma and recovery: The aftermath of violence-from domestic abuse to political terror.* Basic Books.

Klein, M. H., Mathieu, P. L., Gendlin, E. T., & Kiesler, D. J. (1969). *The experi-*

encing scale: A research and training manual. Madison. University of Wisconsin Extension Bureau of Audiovisual Instruction.

Lanius, R. A., Terpou, B. A., & McKinnon, M. C. (2020). The sense of self in the aftermath of trauma: lessons from the default mode network in posttraumatic stress disorder. *European Journal of Psychotraumatology, 11*(1), 1807703–1807703. doi.org/10.1080/20008198.2020.1807703

Lewis, M. (2015). *The biology of desire: Why addiction is not a disease.* PublicAffairs.

Main, M., & Solomon, J. (1990). Procedures for identifying infants as disorganized/disoriented during the Ainsworth Strange Situation. In M. T. Greenberg, D. Cicchetti, & E. M. Cummings (Eds.), *Attachment in the pre-school years: theory, research and intervention* (pp. 121-160). The John D. and Catherine T. MacArthur Foundation Series on mental health and development. Chicago: University of Chicago Press.

Maté, G. (2010). *In the realm of hungry ghosts: Close encounters with addiction.* North Atlantic Books.

Maté, G. (2022). *The myth of normal: Trauma, illness & healing in a toxic culture.* Alfred A. Knopf Canada.

Merrick, M. T., Ford, D. C., Ports, K. A., & Guinn, A. S. (2018). Prevalence of adverse childhood experiences from the 2011-2014 behavioural risk factor surveillance system in 23 states. *JAMA Pediatrics, 172*(11), 1038-1044. doi.org/10.1001/jamapediatrics.2018.2537

Müller, D. (1995). Dealing with self-criticism: The critic within us and the criticized one. *The Folio: A Journal for Focusing and Experiential Psychotherapy, 23*(3), 151–165.

Murray, M. (2012). *The Murray method.* Vivo Publications.

Porges, S. (2011). *The Polyvagal Theory.* Norton.

Porges, S. (2017). *The pocket guide to the Polyvagal Theory: The transformative power of feeling safe.* Norton.

Porges, S. W. (1992). Vagal tone: a physiologic marker of stress vulnerability. *Pediatrics, 90*(3 Pt 2), 498–504. https://pubmed.ncbi.nlm.nih.gov/1513615/

Porges, S. W. (2022). Polyvagal Theory: A science of safety. *Frontiers in integrative neuroscience, 16*, 871227. doi.org/10.3389/fnint.2022.871227

Porges. S. W., & Porges, S. (2023). *Our polyvagal world: How safety and trauma change us.* Norton.

Putnam, F. W. (1989). *Diagnosis and treatment of multiple personality disorder (foundations of modern psychiatry).* Guilford Press.

Schwartz, A. (2024). *Applied Polyvagal Theory in yoga: Therapeutic practices to enhance for emotional health.* Norton.

Schwartz, R. (2019). *Internal family systems therapy* (2nd ed.). Guilford Press.

Siegel, D. J. (1999). *The developing mind: Toward a neurobiology of interpersonal experience.* Guilford Press.

Siegel, D. J. (2010a). *Mindsight: The new science of personal transformation.* Bantam Books.

Siegel, D. J. (2010b). *The mindful therapist.* Norton.

Siegel, D. J. (2012). *Pocket guide to interpersonal neurobiology: An integrative handbook of the mind.* Norton.

Sykes, C., Sweezy, M., & Schwartz, R. (2023) *Internal Family Systems Therapy for addictions: Trauma-informed compassion-based interventions for substance use, eating, gambling, and more.* PesiPublishing.com.

Sykes, C. & Sykes, C. C. (2016). An IFS lens on addiction; compassion for extreme parts. In M. Sweezy & E. L. Ziskind (Eds.), *Innovations and elaborations.* Routledge.

Tajfel, H., & Turner, J. C. (1985) The social identity theory of intergroup behavior. In S. Worchel & W. G. Austin (Eds.), Psychology of intergroup relations (2nd ed., pp. 7–24). Chicago: Nelson-Hall.

Tipple, S. D. (2021). Decolonizing the conceptualization of trauma: An indigenous focusing-oriented approach (master's thesis, University of Calgary, Calgary, Canada). https://prism.ucalgary.ca/server/api/core/bitstreams/868d79f2-d52c-4594-914b-2cd0f6deaff9/content

Van der Kolk, B. A. (2015). *The body keeps the score: Brain, mind, and body in the healing of trauma.* Penguin Books.

Winhall, J. (2021). *Treating trauma and addiction with the felt sense polyvagal model: A bottom-up approach.* Routledge.

Winhall, J., & Porges, S. W. (2022). Revolutionizing addiction treatment with the felt sense polyvagal model. *International Body Psychotherapy Journal, 21*(1), 13–31.

Winhall, J, & Lanius, R. (2024, February 8). *The restoration of the hijacked self.* [Embodied Dialogue Series]. https://www.youtube.com/watch?v=szIv8oOXWOc&list=PL441gpGZmE6sB1rnHhqqieEU85lRixw7l&t=1s

Winhall, J. (2025). The Felt Sense Polyvagal model: Embodied assessment and treatment tool. In H. Grassmann, M. Stupiggia, & S. W. Porges (Eds.), *Somatic-oriented therapies: Embodiment, trauma, and polyvagal perspectives.* Norton.

Wheel of privilege and power. (2023, January 13). Just 1 Voice. Retrieved from https://just1voice.com/advocacy/wheel-of-privilege/

Young, I. (1998). The five faces of oppression. *Philosophical Forum, 19*(4), xix.

Index

Note: Italicized page locators refer to figures; tables are noted with a *t*.

ABC model: Antecedent, Behavior, Consequences (Practice 11), 97–98
abused children, self-harming/self-soothing behaviors and, 20
abusive relationships, 93, 155
accountability, 42–43. *see also* FSPM accountability partnership
ACES. *see* adverse childhood experiences scale (ACES)
action brain (striatum), 95, 98
adaptation
  borderline personality, 144–45, 149
  dissociative identity, 143, 149
addicted brain, 94–96
  amygdala, 96
  dorsolateral prefrontal cortex, 95
  midbrain, 96
  orbitofrontal cortex, 96
  ventral striatum, 95–96
addiction(s)
  as adaptive state regulation strategies, 26, 27

behavioral, 92
being in love *vs.*, 93–94
childhood trauma as underbelly of, 114–115
defining: sick or bad?, 85–87
disorganized attachment style and, 124, 126
dissociation *vs.*, 91–92
hypermasculinity and, 35
intersection of trauma, oppression, and, 113
as a learned habit, 87, 106
neuroplasticity and, 88–89, 107
seeing through polyvagal lens, 25
simple definition of, 23
survival mode and, 86
trauma feedback loop fueled by, 91
see also learning model of addiction
addictive behaviors, making sense of, 97
adverse childhood experiences, Felitti's eight categories of, 118, 120

adverse childhood experiences scale
    (ACES), 115–117, 129
    calculating score for, 120–121, 121t,
        129
    later studies and, 119–120
    paradigm shift: context tells the
        story and, 117
    weight loss program story, 115–117
affairs, 93
Ainsworth, M., 122, 123, 127
Alexander, B., 123
aliveness, heightened sense of, 154
Allison, M., 160, 161, 169
amygdala, as "emotional spray paint," 96
ANS. see autonomic nervous system
    (ANS)
anti-oppressive lens
    bringing to field of attachment the-
        ory, 127
    in Felt Sense Polyvagal Model, 112
Arie, I., 153
asking
    Focusing and, Step 5, 69, 71
    Ian's safe nest: PI focusing oriented
        therapy session, 78
attachment
    authenticity vs., 155–56, 166
    broad categories of, 112
    classifications of, 123–124
    four styles of, 123–124, 129
attachment exercise: healing early
    wounds (Practice 14), 128–129
attachment styles
    mapping Felt Sense Polyvagal Model
        and, 124, 126–127
    relationships and different types of,
        122
attachment theory
    critiquing, 127, 129
    holding and letting go, 121–123

attunement, lack of, 121
Augustine, S., 37
authenticity
    attachment vs., 155–56, 166
    definition of, 155
    expansive nature of, 156
autonomic nervous system (ANS), 23,
    24, 36, 42, 62, 131, 152, 156
    addictive/harmful behaviors and, 100
    addictive shifts in, 73
    four blended states of, 52–53
    healing, Focusing partnership and,
        67
    as main source of healing, 26, 27
    Porges's polyvagal informed, 49
    safety and ventral branch of, 34
    as score keeper, 110, 111
    self-harming behaviors and, 20
    social engagement and, 122
    three main states in, 51
    traditional model of, 48
    understanding behavior through lens
        of, 117

background feeling, 139, 145, 149
Badenoch, B., 145
Bass, E., 19
behavior, persons as being more than, 86
behavioral addictions, 92
binge eating, sexual abuse and, 116
Biology of Desire, The: Why Addiction is
    Not a Brain Disease (Lewis), 87
biology of trauma, understanding, 22
blame, liberating yourself from, 152,
    153, 166, 168
bodily knowing, becoming an expert
    in, 73
body
    finding your way back to your own, 38
    language of, 19, 167

metaphors and, 133
moving with your feelings of expansion, 152–53
as your guide, 110
see also body wisdom
Body Cards. *see* FSPM Body Cards
Body Keeps the Score, The (van der Kolk), 110
body scans, 73
body wisdom, 39, 78
  honoring and trusting in, 58, 59, 88, 109, 140
  Inner Guide and, 141
borderline personality disorder, 149
borderline personality disorder adaptation, 144–45, 149
bottom-up processing, 62
bottom-up right hemisphere experiencing, top-down left hemisphere thinking *vs.*, 167
Bowlby, J., 122, 123
bradycardia, 48–49
brain
  addicted: how good people can do bad things, 94–96
  neuroplasticity of, 87–88
  see also addicted brain
brain patterns, rainwater analogy and, 89–90
brain stem
  neuroception and, 60
  social engagement system and, 61
Brain that Changes Itself, The (Doidge), 88
Butler, S., 144

Carnes, P., 100
celebrating you, as a mixed bag, 164
"Celebration" (Kool and the Gang), 165
Celebration Practice in Three Steps (Practice 20), 165–66

chanting, 58
child abuse, 135, 136
childhood trauma, as underbelly of addiction, 114–115
chocolate, addiction to, Isabella's story about, 135–6, 137, 140
classism, 35
class oppression, 139
Clearing a Space
  Focusing and, Step 1, 68, 69–70, 146
  Ian's safe nest: PI focusing oriented therapy session, 77
Clearing a Space/Clearing the Critic, Step 1 in focusing, 146
Clearing Space Backwards (Practice 17), 147, 149
climate change, 17, 35
cohesive narrative, time and place emerging into, 131
collective nervous system, trauma, safety, and, 35, 36
communities of compassion: flocking and unfolding, 156–62
community violence, 120
compassion
  visiting parts with, 149
  yoga practice and, 159
compassionate community, 156, 166
competence, felt sense of, 152
complex trauma, 35
conflict resolution, 143
connection, 164
  community engagement and, 157
  with others, healing and, 38, 61
  playful coregulation and, 161
  survival and, 155
context tells the story
  Felitti's paradigm shift and, 117
  Isabella's risky ride and, 133–34

coregulation, 62–63
    empowerment feedback loop and,
        166
    Flocking: celebrating your partner-
        ship in, 165
    healing and, 71
    playful, 161
    power of, 157
counting behavior, stopping, 92, 103
Courage to Heal, The (Bass & Davis), 19
COVID-19 pandemic, 17, 35, 58, 139
crayons, 43
creating a safe nest (Practices 1-3),
    33–45
    the Five P's (Practice 1), 39–43, 45
    Noticing the Space Around You
        (Practice 2), 34, 47–48
    The Pause (Practice 3), 44
critic
    to criticized, changing the focus
        from, 148–49
    disarming, 148, 149
    fear and, 147, 148
    using as a signpost, 148, 149
    working with: clearing space,
        145–46
cultural norms, attachment patterns
    and, 123

daily/weekly healing practices, 163–64
Dana, D., 158
dance, 58
Davis, L., 19
decade of the brain (1990s), 22, 85, 87
deepening, fourth circle: Four Circles
    Harm Reduction Practice, 99,
    103–104, 105
default mode network, 154–55, 166
default state, documenting, 110
definitions, power of, 106

desire/wanting
    dopamine and, 95–96
    as prime motivator in addiction, 90,
        93, 95
developmental (or complex) trauma,
    35, 36
diagnosis, making, DSM and, 110
Diagnostic and Statistical Manual
    (DSM), 110
disarming the critic, 148, 149
disease model of addiction, 86
    failure of, 17, 119
    FSPM as challenge to, 27
disorganized attachment style, 122,
    123, 124, 126, 136
disruptor, disarming: note to practi-
    tioners, 147–48
dissociation, 42
    addiction *vs.*, 91–92
    bodily awareness blocked by, 38
dissociative identity adaptation, 143,
    149
dissociative identity disorder, 143, 149
divorce, parental, later ACES study and
    addition of, 119, 120, 121*t*
Doidge, N., 88, 90
dopamine
    midbrain and regulation of, 96
    wanting and, 95–96
dorsal dissociated state, childhood
    trauma and, 131
dorsal vagus, 24, 49, 63
dorsolateral prefrontal cortex (DPC)
    as "the bridge of the ship," 95, 97,
        138, 141
    as your adult responsible self, 105
drawing paper, 43
drum in Mi'kmaw culture, Mother the
    Earth, safety, and heartbeat of, 37,
    127

DSM. *see Diagnostic and Statistical Manual* (DSM)
Dylan, B., 161

EAI. *see* Embodied Ancestral Inquiry (EAI)
EATT. *see Embodied Assessment and Treatment Tool* (Winhall) (EATT)
Embodied Ancestral Inquiry (EAI), 160, 169
Embodied Assessment and Treatment Tool (Winhall) (EATT), 110
Embodied Dialogues, 158
embodied knowing, welcome to, 74
embodied liberation, 168
embodiment, trauma assessment and treatment and, 110
emergency meetings, 164
emotional abuse
    ACEs score and, 121*t*
    recurrent and severe, 118
emotional regulation, diagnoses viewed through lens of, 22
empowerment feedback loop, *50,* 166
    healing and, 152–53
    shifting into, 163
Experiencing Scale (Gendlin), 74–76, 83
    dorsal states: Levels 1 and 2, 75
    example of, 75
    Ian's safe nest: PI focusing oriented therapy session, 76, 77, 78
    sympathetic states: Levels 3 and 4, 76
    ventral states: Levels 1–7, 75
eye contact, 61

Favoring Others for Survival state (FSPM), *50*
    description of, 53

insecure attachment blended state and, 124, 126
    as a state of hyperarousal, 54
Fawning and Favoring Others for Survival, *50,* 156
FCHRP. *see* Four Circles Harm Reduction Practice (FCHRP)
fear, critic and, 147, 148
feedback loops
    neurons that fire together, wire together, 89–90, 152
    ubiquity of, 91
    see also empowerment feedback loop; trauma feedback loop
Felitti, V., 115, 116, 117, 118, 119, 129
felt sense, 21
    background part of, 139
    of Focusing partnership, 165
    of neuroception (Practice 5), 59–60, 156
    of the safe nest (Practice 7), 73–74
    of your experience, integration and, 167
    of your gut feelings, 155
Felt Sense Polyvagal Community, 158, 166
Felt Sense Polyvagal Facilitators, 158
Felt Sense/Polyvagal Grounding Practice (FSPGP), 79–80
Felt Sense Polyvagal Model (FSPM), 21, 23, 37, 65, 86, 87, 119
    accountability and, 42–43
    anti-oppressive lens in, 112
    autonomic nervous system as basis for, 110
    as a body friendly map, 55
    body wisdom and, 39
    borderline parts welcomed in, 144
    clinician version, 55, *56,* 74, *125*

Felt Sense Polyvagal Model (FSPM)
    (*continued*)
    communities connected with,
        157–62
    five theories in, 18, 27, 121
    foundation of, 20
    four core concepts in, 26, 27
    graphic version of, introducing, 49
    integrated into Four Circles Harm
        Reduction Practice, 100, *101, 102*
    interoception/neuroception and,
        25–26, 65–66
    listening to the language of the body
        and, 167
    many models for working with parts
        and, 145
    mapping attachment styles and, 124,
        126–127
    primary source of healing in, 17
    safety as bedrock in, 33–34
    7 F states in, *50,* 51–55
Felt Sense Polyvagal Trauma/Addiction
    Groups, 158
felt shift, 21–22
    at heart of Focusing, 72–73
    as shift in the ANS, 26, 27, 34
    see also felt sense
feminist and trauma-informed theory,
    18, 28, 121
fight/flight/freeze response, amygdala
    and, 23, 93, 95, 96
Fight/Flight state (FSPM), *50,* 52, 54
Finding Focusing, 66
Finding the Felt Sense (Practice 6)
    Focusing and, Step 2, 69, 70, 82
    Ian's safe nest: PI focusing oriented
        therapy session, 77
    six steps of focusing, 69–72
First Memories of Feeling Soothed
    (Practice 10), 94, 127

Fisher, J., 145
Five P's
    pacing, 39, 40, 45, 109, 162
    partnership, 39, 41–43, 45
    pausing and triggers, 39, 40–41, 45
    place and time, 39–40, 45
    presence, 39, 43, 45
Fixate/Freeze/Fawn state (FSPM), *50,*
    53, 54
Flocking: Celebrating Your Partnership
    in Coregulation, in Celebration
    Practice in Three Steps (Practice
    20), 165
Flock state (FSPM), *50,* 51, 54, 61,
    152, 155
Flowing, Flock, Fun, Fired Up: Drop-
    ping Down Inside
    in Celebration Practice in Three
        Steps (Practice 20), 165
flowing, secure attachment blended
    state and, 126
Flowing state (FSPM), *50, 53*
fMRIs, xx
Focusing, 65, 121
    alone, 68
    as a contemplative practice, 66, 67
    felt shift at heart of, 72–73
    interoception and, 58
    power of, 158
Focusing (Gendlin), 66
Focusing, Gendlin's six steps of, 22,
    68–72
    asking, 69, 71
    clearing a space, 68, 69–70, 146
    finding a felt sense, 69, 70, 82
    getting a handle, 69, 70
    resonating, 69, 71
    welcoming or receiving, 69, 71–72
Focusing/Felt Sensing, 18, 21–22,
    27

Focusing Initiatives International, 159,
    169
Focusing Institute, 158
Focusing Oriented Psychotherapy (Gend-
    lin), 66
Focusing partnerships
    as coregulating practice, 66–67
    guidelines for, 67–68
    power of, 71
Fold/Fawn/Fixate/Freeze/Flight/
    Fight, insecure/Disorganized
    blended state and, 124, 126
Fold state (FSPM), *50, 52,* 54
Four Circles Harm Reduction Practice
    (FCHRP), 25, 109, 162, 163
    daily check-ins, 106
    example, *102*
    fourth circle: deepening, 99, 103–
        104, 105
    handouts, 43
    inner circle: letting go, 99, 100, 103,
        104
    as a roadmap for healing, 99–105
    second circle: triggering, 99, 103,
        104
    third circle: grounding, 99, 103, 104
Four Circles Harm Reduction Practice
    (Practice 12), 104–105, 107
fragmented selves, working with, 145
Frankl, V., 37
FSPGP. *see* Felt Sense/Polyvagal
    Grounding Practice (FSPGP)
FSPM. *see* Felt Sense Polyvagal Model
    (FSPM)
FSPM Accountability Partner, around
    the clock support and, 164
FSPM Accountability Partnership,
    beginning, 105, 107
FSPM Body Cards, 133, 94, 98, 104,
    129, 142, 146, 162, 163, 165

addiction body card, example, *80*
    development of, 80
    making your own, 82
    Process Recording and, 81–82, 83
    two separate Focusing sessions,
        examples of, 81
Fun/Fired Up, *50, 52*
    Moving to Music, in Celebration
        Practice in Three Steps (Practice
        20), 165
    secure attachment blended state
        and, 126

gender oppression, 139
Gendlin, E. T., 21, 22, 34, 37, 59, 60,
    66, 68, 72, 74, 82, 83, 90, 139,
    141, 159
getting a handle
    Focusing and, Step 3, 69, 70
    Ian's safe nest: PI focusing oriented
        therapy session, 78
global trauma, 58, 139
goals, addiction and, 95, 96, 97
graphic images, bodily experience and,
    51
graphic model, as a visual roadmap,
    55
Greatest Night in Pop, The, 161
grief, 97
grounded sense of self, 72
grounding, third circle: Four Circles
    Harm Reduction Practice, 99,
    103, 104
gut feelings, connecting with, 155

habits, feedback loops and, 90
harm reduction, shaping treatment
    plan for, 99. *see also* Four Cir-
    cles Harm Reduction Practice
    (FCHRP)

healing
    connection with others and, 38, 61
    coregulation and, 71
    creative ways of finding safety and,
        36–38
    daily/weekly practices for, 163
    integration and, 142
    lifelong journey of, 151
    reclaiming your power and, 152
    safety and, 156
    three stages of, 20, 109
    see also Four Circles Harm Reduc-
        tion Practice (FCHRP)
Hebb, D. O., 90
Heinrich, M., 160
Hendricks-Gendlin, M., 158
Herman, J., 20, 25, 109, 112, 129, 151,
    166
heteronormativity, 35
hope, intention and, 38–39
housing insecurity, 120
hypermasculinity, 35

"I Am Light" (Arie), 153
I am Light: Moments of Liberation
    (Practice 18), 153
incest, 144
Inner Community Work, 145
Inner Family Systems, 145
Inner Guide, 143, 148, 152, 164
    authentic self and, 155
    body wisdom and, 141
    borderline parts and, 144
    embodied practices and, 167
    finding whole sense of self and,
        153–54
    invitation to, 142
    managing the critic without fear
        and, 147

insecure/ambivalent attachment style,
    Ainsworth's research on, 123, 124
insecure attachment style
    blended states and, 126
    family constellations and, 122
insecure/avoidant attachment style,
    Ainsworth's research on, 123–124
integration, 99
    felt sense of your experience and,
        167
    note about, 142–43
    reflection and, 163
integrity
    living a life of, 86
    losing connection with, 95
intention, hope and, 38–39
intergenerational trauma, 136, 139,
    160
internal critic, working with: clearing
    space, 145–46
International Focusing Institute, 158–
    59, 169
interoception, 73, 82, 99, 100, 109,
    167
    definition of, 65
    Felt Sense Polyvagal Model and,
        25–26, 27
    polyvagal approach to, 58–59, 63
Interpersonal Neurobiology (IPNB),
    18, 22, 27, 121–122, 124, 129
In the Realm of Hungry Ghosts: Close
    Encounters with Addiction (Maté), 91
IPNB. see interpersonal neurobiology
    (IPNB)
Isabella
    building a safe nest, 132–3
    critic within: the vice, 136–7
    finding and working with parts,
        140–41

grandmother's chocolate love, 136
parts of: the hungry one, the little
    one, and the thief, 134–5
pausing and reflecting on story of,
    137–8
risky ride: context tells the story,
    133–4
isolation, 42

Jones, Q., 161
journals, 43
joy, 43, 164

language of the body, power of, 19
Lanius, R., 153, 154, 166
learning model of addiction, 19, 23,
    27, 87, 88–89, 93, 106
letting go, inner circle: Four Circles
    Harm Reduction Practice, 99,
    100, 103, 104
Lewis, M., 23, 87, 88, 89, 93, 95, 96,
    106, 107
liberation
    embodied, 168
    exploring felt sense of, 152–53
    feeling into small moments of, 152
loneliness, 42
love addiction, 93
lying, 42, 43

macro aggressions, 113
Main, M., 123
Making Your FSPM Body Cards (Prac-
    tice 9), 82
marginalization, 35, 112, 114
Maté, G., 91, 111, 114, 115, 155, 156,
    166
medical model, 110
meditation, 105

memory(ies)
    dorsal dissociated state and gaps in,
        131
    retrieval of, note about, 140
    safety and surfacing of, 133
    somatic, 93
Merrick, M., 119, 120
Merzenich, M., 88
metaphors, body and communicating
    in, 133
micro aggressions, 113
midbrain, as dopamine pump, 96
Middle East, war in, 35
Mi'kmaq Creation Story, 37
Mi'kmaw culture, secure attachment
    and safety in, 127
mind/body connection, honoring,
    interoception and, 58–59, 60
mindsight, 22, 121–122
misogyny, 35
moderation, practicing, 90
moral failure model, 86, 106
Mother Nature, finding spiritual con-
    nection to, 36–37
movement, mobilizing through, 161
Müller, D., 148
Multiple Personality Theory, 145
Murray, M., 138
music, moving to, 165
myelination, of ventral vagus, 49
Myth of Normal, The (Maté), 155

natural disasters, 120
neuroception, 65, 69, 72, 73, 99, 100,
    109, 111, 155, 167
    faulty, 60
    Felt Sense of (Practice 5), 59–60, 156
    Felt Sense Polyvagal Model and,
        25–26, 27

neuroception (*continued*)
  polyvagal approach to, 59–60, 63
  power of, 24
neurons that fire together, wire
    together, 90, 105, 152
neuropathways, new and healthy, cre-
    ating, 121
neuroplasticity, 23
  addiction and, 88–89, 107
  constantly changing brain and,
    87–88
Noticing the Space Around You (Prac-
    tice 2), 44, 47–48, 69
numbing, 38, 85

OFC. *see* orbitofrontal cortex (OFC)
oppression, 35
  intersection of trauma, addiction,
    and, 113
  trauma and systems of, 119
orbitofrontal cortex (OFC), as connec-
    tor, 96
organization links, 169
organized attachment patterns, 122

pacing (Five P's), 39, 40, 45, 109, 162,
    164
parental separation or divorce, later
    ACES study and addition of, 119,
    120, 121t
partnership (Five P's), 39, 41–43, 45
parts
  borderline personality adaptation
    and, 144–45
  dissociative identity adaptation and,
    143
  finding and working with, 140–41
  lost, living with, 140
  many models for working with, 145
  visiting with compassion, 149

  welcoming inner diversity of,
    142–43
  working with, Practice 46, 142
Parts Body Cards, 142
Pause, The (Practice 3), 44
pausing, connection and, 38
pausing and triggers (Five P's), 39,
    40–41, 45
pet scans, 22
physical abuse
  ACEs score and, 121t
  recurrent and severe, 118
place and time (Five P's), 39–40, 45
planning ahead, 38
plastic paradox, 105
  lack of felt sense and, 90
  love addiction and, 93
play, embodied healing of trauma and,
    160–61
Polyvagal Informed Focusing, 72
polyvagal informed (PI) focusing ori-
    ented therapy session: Ian's safe
    nest, 76–79, 83
  asking, 78
  clearing a space, 77
  finding a felt sense: Experience Scale
    3 to 4, 77–78
  getting a handle: Experience Scale 4
    to 5, 78
  resonating, 78
  swaying and swerving handle, 77, 78
  welcoming: Experience scale 6 to 7,
    78–79
Polyvagal Informed Yoga Community,
    159
Polyvagal Institute, 157–58, 161, 169
polyvagal paradigm shift, 152
Polyvagal Play Zone, 160–62
Polyvagal Theory, 18, 20, 23–26, 27,
    48, 52, 58, 63, 65, 100, 121, 157

Polyvagal Theory, five lessons in, 57–63
    coregulation, 62–63
    interoception, 58–59, 63
    neuroception, 59–60, 63
    safety first, 57–58, 63
    social engagement, 61–62, 63
Porges, S., 20, 23, 24, 26, 34, 48, 49,
    59, 60, 61, 62, 63, 65, 155, 157,
    158
poverty, 35
power, intersection of privilege and,
    113, 114
Practice Recording forms, downloads
    for, 43
prayer, 105
prefrontal cortex, 96, 155
presence (Five P's), 39, 43, 45
privilege, intersection of power and,
    113, 114
Process Recordings, 74, 80, 81–82, 83,
    94, 98, 110, 128–129, 142, 162,
    163, 165
pruning, 93
purpose, finding, 37–38
Putnam, F., 145

race, 139
racism, 35
rainwater analogy, brain patterns and,
    89–90
Recognizing/Retuning Your Nervous
    System States, 53, 110
reconnection, 20, 109, 151, 166
Redfield, R., 157
reflect, digest, make a plan, 162
reflecting, Embodied Timeline and,
    162–63
reinforcement, habits, addiction, and,
    90
relationship addiction, 93

remembering and mourning, 20, 109,
    129, 133, 149, 164
repetition
    increased, plastic paradox and, 90
    as a resource, 45, 47
    wiring of the brain and, 88
resonating
    Focusing and, Step 4, 69, 71
    Ian's safe nest: PI focusing oriented
        therapy session, 78
Richard Schwartz Internal Family Sys-
    tems model, 145
right hemisphere of brain, graphic
    models and, 51
Rogers, C., 21
rumination, 96

safe nest, building, 132–3
safe place inside of yourself, finding,
    36
safe relationships, establishing, chal-
    lenges with, 122
safety, 25, 72, 100
    ANS and sense of, 26
    authenticity, attachment, and, 155
    as the bedrock, 33–34
    changing definitions of, 35–36
    cues of, 61
    empowerment feedback loop and,
        152
    establishing, 20, 109
    felt shift and, 21
    finding, creative ways for, 36–38
    healing and, 156
    integration and, 143
    moment-by-moment, finding, 37
    neuroplasticity and, 23
    prioritizing, in healing journey, 20
    reconnection and, 151
    surfacing of memories and, 133

safety first, polyvagal approach, 57–58,
     63
Schwartz, A., 159, 169
Schwartz, R., 145
secure attachment style, 35, 122
     Ainsworth's research on, 123
     blended states and, 126
     cultural awareness about, 127
     trauma feedback loop and absence
          of, 122
self care, daily/weekly practices and,
     153
self-compassion, 86
self-harm, seeing through polyvagal
     lens, 25
self-harming/self-soothing behaviors,
     paradoxical behavior of survivors
     and, 20
self-regulation, attachment theory and,
     122
self-soothing, early memories of, 94,
     107
7 F states, Felt Sense Polyvagal Model,
     50, 51–55, 110, 162, 163
     Favoring Others for Survival, 50,
          53, 54
     Fight/Flight, 50, 52, 54
     Fixate/Freeze/Fawn, 50, 53, 54
     Flock, 50, 51, 54
     Flowing, 50, 53
     Fold, 50, 52, 54
     Fun/Fired Up, 50, 52, 54
sexual abuse, 118
     ACEs score and, 121t
     binge eating and, 116
     weight gain as survival strategy and,
          116, 117
shame, 86
     healing, 42
     inner critic and, 145

liberating yourself from, 152, 153,
     166, 168
sickness model, 85, 89, 106
Siegel, D., 22, 121, 122, 124, 129
sobriety, achieving, 105
sobriety model, 100
social connection as a biological imper-
     ative (Porges), 155, 157
social engagement, 61–63, 122
     empowerment feedback loop and,
          152
     trauma feedback loop and, 61–62
social engagement system, 42, 61
     default mode network and, 154
     Focusing and, 67, 68
social identity theory, 113
social movement of liberation
     supporting for all, 112
     trauma survivors and, 157
Solomon, J., 123
somatic memories, formation of, 93
soothing behaviors, 93
spiritual bypassing, 105
SSP. see strange situation procedure
     (SSP)
stealing behavior, linking to memory
     of Nona's chocolate love, 135–6,
     137, 140
stepping out into the world, 152
strange situation procedure (SSP), 123
stress, activated voice of the critic and,
     148
striatum (Motivational Engine), 138
support, 24-hour, 164
survival
     connection and, 155
     of the fittest, 62
     mode, addictions occurring in, 86
Sweezy, M., 145
Sykes, C., 145

sympathetic nervous system
  evolution of, 61
  music and, 165

Tajfel, H., 113
taking up space, meaning of and steps
    to take for, 152
text messaging, 164
TFL. *see* trauma feedback loop (TFL)
therapy process, titrating, three-stage
    model in, 20
threat
  default mode network and, 154
  reducing, 38
Three Circle Exercise, 100
tone of voice, 61
top-down left hemisphere thinking,
    bottom-up right hemisphere
    experiencing *vs.*, 167
top-down processing, 62
training, through Polyvagal Institute, 158
trauma
  addictive behaviors and, 114–115
  assessing, 110
  being stuck in the past and, 154
  biology of, understanding, 22
  changing definitions of, 35–36
  constricting nature of, 156
  context tells the story of, 117
  defining, 111
  global nature of, 35, 36, 58, 139
  intergenerational, 136, 139, 160
  intersection of addiction, oppres-
    sion, and, 113
  lost sense of self after, 153
  self-power robbed by, 152
  systems of oppression and, 119
Trauma Egg, 137, 149, 163
  adding new information to, 140
  background feelings and, 139

creation of, 138
different parts of yourself and, 141
making, 138–9
Practice 45, 139–10
trauma feedback loop (TFL), 25, 27,
    34, 52, 58, 103, 107, 133, 152,
    154, 155
  absence of secure attachment and, 122
  addictive shift and, 73
  as ANS back-up plan, 91
  being stuck in, 42
  borderline personality adaptation
    and, 144
  dorsal numbing state and, 117
  faulty neuroception and, 60
  social engagement and, 61–62
  triggers and, 41
Trauma Theory, 121
traumatic tension, 156
*Treating Trauma and Addiction with the
    Felt Sense Polyvagal Model* (Win-
    hall), 18
triggering, second circle: Four Circles
    Harm Reduction Practice, 99,
    103, 104
triggers
  pausing and, 40–41
  reframing your view of, 41
trust, 43. *see also* safety
trusting relationships, self-regulation
    and, 122
Turner, J., 113
twelve-step model, Four Circles Harm
    Reduction Practice *vs.*, 100
twenty embodied practices, 26, 27

Ugandan culture, first ACE studies
    and, 127
Ukraine war, 35
uncomfortable feelings, honoring, 21

vagal paradox, resolution of, 48–49
vagus nerve, 58, 65, 95
    as brain/body connector, 23–24
    discrete motor branches of, 49
    threat and ventral branch of, 34
    ventral branch of, 24, 25
van der Kolk, B., 110
ventral energy, social engagement and,
    122
ventral regulation, Body Cards and
    neural exercise of, 82
ventral striatum (VS), as motivational
    engine, 95–96
ventral vagus
    color images and, 51
    Porges's paradox and, 48–49
violence, community, 120
VS. *see* ventral striatum (VS)
vulnerability, 148

wanting. *see* desire/wanting
war, 17
"We Are the World," 161
weight gain, as survival strategy, 117
welcoming, Ian's safe nest: PI focusing
    oriented therapy session, 78–79
welcoming or receiving, Focusing and,
    Step 6, 69, 71–72

welcoming space, creating, 112
Wheel of Awareness, The, 122
Wheel of Privilege (Practice 13), 113,
    129, 160
    Erased group in, 114
    Marginalized group in, 114
    Power group in, 114
    reflecting on, 119
white culture, first ACE studies and, 127
white supremacy, 160
whole sense of self, finding, 153–54
Wonder, S., 161
Working with Parts (Practice 16), 142,
    149
wounded child, connecting with, 148
wounded place, making a caring rela-
    tionship with, 128–129

yoga
    combining with FSPM Daily Prac-
        tices, 159
    Focusing and, 58
Young, I., 112, 113
Your Embodied Timeline: Review and
    Reflect (Practice 19), 166
    more rounds of, 163
    Step One, 162
    Step Two, 163

About the Author

Jan Winhall, MSW, PIFOT, is an author, teacher, and seasoned trauma and addiction psychotherapist. She is an educational partner with the Polyvagal Institute where she offers a two-year training program based on her book *Treating Trauma and Addiction with the Felt Sense Polyvagal Model* (Routledge, 2021). Her book *20 Embodied Practices for Healing Trauma and Addiction: Using the Felt Sense Polyvagal Model* (Norton, 2025) is a guide for therapists and clients to implement the Felt Sense Polyvagal Model. Jan and her trainers offer groups for clients to heal together using the 20 embodied practices. She has created a somatic assessment tool that is described in her chapter in *Somatic-Oriented Therapies: Embodiment, Trauma, and Polyvagal Perspectives* (Norton, 2025). She is an adjunct lecturer at the University of Toronto and a certifying coordinator with the International Focusing Institute. She is also the codirector of the Borden Street Clinic where she supervises graduate students. Jan enjoys teaching all over the world. You can reach her at janwinhall.com.